The Theatregoer's Cookbook

Victorian music sheet cover.

The Theatregoer's Cookbook

Catherine Haill

Threshold Books

'Sit down and feed, and welcome to our table'

As You Like It Act I, scene vii

For May and Leslie.
And Jonathan who ate it all —
several times.

Published by Threshold Books Limited
661 Fulham Road, London SW6 5PZ

© 1986 Catherine Haill

Designed by Kirby-Sessions Design.

Printed by Thomson Litho, Glasgow.

All rights reserved

No part of this publication may be reproduced, stored in a
retrieval system, or transmitted, in any form or by any means,
electronic, mechanical, photocopying, recording, or otherwise,
without written permission of the publisher.

British Library Cataloguing in Publication Data
Haill, Catherine
   The theatre-goer's cookbook.
   1. Cookery, International
   I. Title
   641.5   TX725.A1
   ISBN 0–901366–14–5

Special thanks are due to Tony Latham, who kindly checked the
theatre research, and to Jenny and John Jenkins who chose the wines.
   Thanks also to Catherine Ashmore, Ian Beck, Susan Blow, Graham
Brandon, Rexton Bunnett, Charles Castle, Sally Chappell, Paula
Chesterman, Bamber Gascoigne, Joan Hirst, Joanna Holmburg, Rupert
Kirby, Tanya Moiseiwitsch, Alexander Schouvaloff, Veronica Wald,
and all my friends who encouraged and helped me, and ate my
experiments.
   I am grateful to Sheridan Morley, who liked the idea, and to Barbara
Cooper and Threshold for making it possible.

Contents

Introduction	9	Shephard's Pie	75
The Cocktail Party	12	Little Lambs Eat Ivy	78
Don't Start Without Me	19	The Wild Duck	81
Cool as a Cucumber	22	Ever Green	85
In the Soup	26	The Late Christopher Bean	89
The Butter and Egg Man	28	The Magic Cabbage	93
The Apple Cart	30	Goodbye, Mr Chips	95
Share My Lettuce	33	Roots	96
The Amorous Prawn	36	Salad Days	99
Bonne Soupe	38	Bitter Sweet	105
Fish Out of Water	41	The Chocolate Soldier	108
The Goldfish	44	Banana Ridge	110
Albert Herring	47	Oranges and Lemons	113
Big Fish, Little Fish	51	Pineapple Poll	116
Mother Goose	55	A Taste of Honey	119
Pork Chops	59	The Love of Three Oranges	120
The Spring Chicken	63	Bubbling Brown Sugar	123
The Pigeon	66	The Cherry Orchard	125
Turkey Time	69		
Red Peppers	72		

The Recipes

Before Dinner

Dips	14
Canapés	15
Savouries	16

Starters

Ginger chicken	20
Hot breads (garlic, herb, anchovy)	20
Melba toast	21
Mayonnaise	21
Stuffed cucumber	25
Apple, celery and onion soup	27
Creamy egg tartlets	29
Savoury apple starter	31
Lettuce soup	34
Whisky prawn avocado	37
Carrot and yogurt soup	39

Fish

Salmon trout with apple and nut stuffing	43
Smoked haddock pie	45
Stuffed herring with caper sauce	49
Creamy sole with prawns	53

Meat Dishes

Goose with apricot stuffing	57
Cheesy cider chops	61
Chicken with grape sauce	65
Pigeons in cider	67
Turkey fillets in sherry	71

Stuffed peppers	73
Shepherd's pie	77
Lamb chops en croûte	79
Mallard with Cointreau and cream sauce	83

Vegetables

Spinach roulade with onion filling	87
French beans with tomatoes	91
Cabbage with bacon	93
Potatoes au gratin	95
Carrots with watercress	97

Salads

Lettuce, avocado and bacon salad	101
Potato and blue cheese salad	101
Rice, chicken and grape salad	102
Carrot, cheese and orange salad	103
Potato mountain salad	103

Desserts/Puddings

Almond ice cream with raspberry sauce	107
Chocolate mint dessert	109
Baked bananas with coconut	111
Orange and lemon cheesecake	115
Pineapple soufflé	117
Whisky and honey whip	119
Orange cream pie	121
Burnt sugar apricots	123
Drunken cherry ice cream with hot sauce	127

List of wines available at the
Oxford Music Hall, London 1880.

Introduction

Theatre-going and eating out are two of the most pleasurable pastimes in which I regularly indulge. My interest in the theatre began early, and I remember as a child of eight naming my hamster Frederic after the character in *The Pirates of Penzance* of whom the Major General's daughters said: 'How pitiful his tale, how rare his beauty.' Childhood also introduced me to the fun of cooking when my parents gave me a miniature cookery set complete with a quarter-size rolling pin, a real ceramic bowl and an imaginative rhyming cookery book. This disguised otherwise boring but necessary advice in verse which I still remember: 'Opening oven doors – beware!, Stand back to dodge the mad hot air, Or you'll cook you – a sad mistake, If you set out to bake a cake.' Years later, working in the Theatre Museum, it was perhaps inevitable that the two interests should connect. When indexing a programme for a production of *The Amorous Prawn*, it occurred to me to be an apt name for an alcoholic concoction of prawns in sour cream and whisky nestling in a bed of avocado. The title of the Musical *Bubbling Brown Sugar* perfectly describes the result of grilling brown sugar sprinkled on top of frozen cream and apricots; thus the idea took hold of me and more titles of plays inspired more dishes. The plays, the authors, the actors and the theatres are also of interest – some well known and others more obscure – so I decided to write about them both.

In many ways, meals and theatrical performances are similar. The preparation time of each is disproportionately long when compared with the time it takes to eat a meal or to see a show. But just as actors should enjoy the weeks of rehearsal, so a cook should enjoy the preparation of a meal. Complicated cooking every day would make this impossible – and in any case few people would have time for it. Working full time, I am a great believer in quick and easy meals during the week with the 'special' meals reserved for weekends when there is time to enjoy a couple of hours in the kitchen, perhaps tasting a glass of wine as you work. Then cooking becomes a pleasure, as it should be, and not a chore.

The presentation of a dinner party should also be theatrical, seemingly produced with consummate ease by the host or hostess – often testing acting abilities to the full! Guests can feel very uncomfortable when the host makes it plain that the evening has cost a week of cursing in the kitchen, yet even so the sauce has curdled. For a really relaxing party everything should appear serene once the guests arrive; the cutlery, the glasses, the napkins, the flowers and the candles set the scene. Act I is the starter; Act II the fish or meat course, with an interval for cheese and biscuits. I like to serve the dessert as an indulgent Act III after the cheese, since people can rarely resist a dessert; if offered the cheese afterwards they proclaim themselves 'too full'. Try it – it never fails! And for the Afterpiece, in the best Victorian style, coffee with mints and brandy or liqueurs should be savoured at leisure with a satisfied feeling of well-being.

Decorative cartouche from Daly's Theatre programme, 1896, featuring the initials of the theatre manager, Augustin Daly.

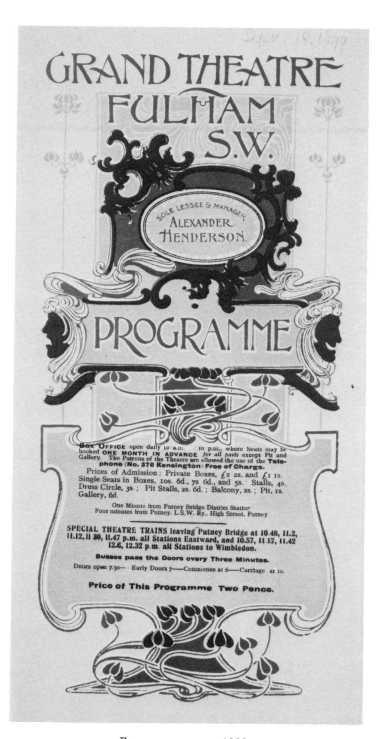

Programme cover, 1899.

Cartoon by Griff, 1950.

The Cocktail Party

With a distinguished cast including Rex Harrison, Donald Houston, Ian Hunter, Alison Leggatt and Margaret Leighton, *The Cocktail Party* opened in London at the New Theatre (now the Albery) on 3 May 1950, having previously been seen at the Edinburgh Festival in August 1949 with Alec Guinness as the Unidentified Guest. Irene Worth remembers her first reading of the play:

'I was so excited by the sound of such exquisitely chosen words, as well as by the rhythmic pattern of the lines, that I expressed an earnest desire to be in the production, even if I had no more to do than carry on a teacup.'

In fact she was given the part of Celia Coplestone for the Edinburgh production, when Ernest Clark played Alexander Gibbs. Margaret Leighton and Robin Bailey first played these parts in London, and Miss Worth and Mr Clark played Celia and Alex in the Broadway production in January 1950. Returning to London, they replaced Miss Leighton and Mr Bailey the following August.

The author of *The Cocktail Party*, T.S. Eliot, was born in the USA in 1885 and settled in London in 1914, becoming a British citizen in 1927. Considered a major poet by 1920, he wrote his first play *The Rock* in 1934. He established himself as a poetic dramatist with *Murder In The Cathedral*, 1935, and *The Family Reunion*, 1939, the latter based on Greek myth, as is *The Cocktail Party*.

Disguising Euripides' *Alcestis* as a drawing-room comedy, *The Cocktail Party* is ostensibly about comtemporary sophisticated society, but as the characters talk to the central figure, the psychiatrist Sir Henry Harcourt-Reilly, it becomes evident that on a deeper level the play is about the search for spiritual values in the modern world.

A success in London and New York, the poetry of *The Cocktail Party* is less lyrical than much of Eliot's earlier dramatic writing. The flowing verse often sounds like prose, and includes some wonderfully wry cocktail-party comments, such as Julia's:

'Edward, it's been a delightful evening:
The potato crisps were really excellent'

– and her more honest assessment of Edward and the party:

'What a host! And nothing fit to eat!
The only reason for a cocktail party
For a gluttenous old woman like me
Is a really nice tit-bit. I can drink at home.
Edward, give me another of those delicious olives.
What's that? Potato crisps? No, I can't endure them.'

A recent revival of *The Cocktail Party* by the New Theatre Company opened at the Phoenix Theatre in July 1986. Starring Rachel Kempson, Alec McCowan, Sheila Gish, Sheila Allen, Simon Ward and Stephen Boxer, it featured an elegant Art Déco apartment setting designed by Brian Vahey. Despite critical doubts about the dated feel of verse drama in the 1980s, individual performances were praised. It was the first time the play had been seen in the West End since a production at Wyndhams Theatre in 1968, and as Milton Shulman decided in his review:

'it is the irrelevant, badgering chit-chat of a Martini society that still retains some sparkle.'

Cocktail Party

'A really nice tit-bit' is a memorable part of any drinks party, and although some are time-consuming to prepare, they can be made well in advance and kept fresh in a cool place with a covering of cling-film. Use pumpernickel, rye or white or brown bread for the canapés, as biscuit-based savouries become soft very quickly. Serve all cocktail snacks in small portions to make consumption easier.

Dips

Dips are very easy to make, and are always popular. Serve with a selection of fresh vegetables, cleaned and prepared into individual 'dip-sticks'. Strips of celery, carrot, green, red and white peppers, whole button mushrooms, cauliflower florettes and sliced red or white cabbage leaves are ideal.

Onion Dip

4 oz (100 g) cream cheese
4 oz (100 g) curd cheese
½ packet dried onion soup
3 tablespoons (3 × 15 ml spoons) natural yogurt

Combine the cream cheese and curd cheese in a mixing bowl. Add the yoghurt and the dried onion soup. Stir well and leave for at least 2 hours for the flavours to develop.

Blue Cheese Dip

4 oz (100 g) cream cheese
4 oz (100 g) curd cheese
3 tablespoons (3 × 15 ml spoons) natural yogurt
4 oz (100 g) Danish blue cheese
2 cloves garlic
black pepper

Combine the cream cheese and curd cheese in a mixing bowl. Add the yogurt. Grate the cheese and peel and crush the garlic. Add to the cheese mixture. Stir well and season with black pepper to taste.

Avocado Dip

Using the recipe and method for Blue Cheese Dip, but instead of the blue cheese use the mashed flesh of two avocados and the juice of ½ a lemon.

Cartoon by Griff, 1950.

Canapés

A canapé is literally a savoury on fried bread but I prefer to use pumpernickel, rye or brown or white bread cut into small squares or stamped with a small pastry cutter into rounds. Top with one of the following mixtures and decorate with a sliver of anchovy: a prawn, half a grape, a ring of stuffed olive, a scrap of smoked salmon, a little lumpfish roe, or a small piece of red or green pepper.

Basic cream cheese topping

4 oz (100 g) cream cheese **salt**
8 oz (225 g) curd cheese **black pepper**

Combine the cream cheese and the curd cheese in a mixing bowl and season to taste. Spoon a little mixture on to the prepared canapé bases and decorate as desired.

(Makes about 60 canapés)

Tomato cream cheese topping

Add a teaspoon of tomato purée to the basic cream cheese mixture.

Carrot and cream cheese topping

8 oz (225 g) carrots **small bunch of parsley**
4 oz (100 g) cream cheese **salt, black pepper**

Scrape and slice the carrots then boil them in salted water for 15 minutes. Drain, and allow to cool. Liquidise with the cream cheese. Chop the parsley and add to the cream cheese and carrot mixture. Season to taste and refrigerate until set. Spoon a little mixture on to the prepared canapé bases and decorate as desired.

Savouries

Celery Boats

Wash and dry a head of celery and cut into small 'boats'. Fill with any of the topping mixtures suggested for the canapés and decorate as for the canapés.

Peanut chicken sticks

2 chicken breasts, off the bone
2 tablespoons (2 × 15 ml spoons) peanut butter
1 tablespoon (1 × 15 ml spoon) clear honey
4 tablespoons (4 × 15 ml spoons) ground nut or olive oil
1 teaspoon (1 × 5 ml spoon) soy sauce
½ teaspoon (½ × 5 ml spoon) chilli powder
salt
black pepper

Combine the peanut butter, honey, oil, soy sauce, salt and pepper in a mixing bowl. Slice the chicken breasts into very fine slices. Skewer them on to a cocktail stick and wrap round, skewering the end of the strip on to the end of the stick. Leave all the chicken-wrapped sticks in the marinade, preferably overnight. Preheat a grill until very hot and grill the chicken sticks for about 5 minutes, turning once, until bubbling and golden. They may be served hot or cold.

(Makes about 36 sticks)

Asparagus Pinwheels

1 large tin asparagus spears
½ loaf sliced brown bread
butter
salt
black pepper

Cut the crusts from the brown bread and cut each slice in half, lengthwise. Flatten each piece of bread with a rolling pin and butter each piece sparingly. Season with salt and pepper. Roll an asparagus spear in each piece of bread, like rolling a swiss roll. Wrap all the asparagus rolls in silver foil and refrigerate. Before serving, remove from refrigerator and cut each roll into about 6 pinwheels.

(Makes about 120 pinwheels)

Blue Cheese Straws

6 oz (175 g) plain flour
3 oz (75 g) butter
4 oz (100 g) Danish blue cheese
juice of ½ lemon
2 tablespoons (2 × 15 ml) cold water
salt
black pepper

Sieve the flour with a pinch of salt into a bowl and add the butter, cut into small pieces. Rub the fat into the flour with the fingertips until the mixture resembles breadcrumbs. Grate the cheese into the bowl and season with a little black pepper. Add the water and lemon juice into the centre of the mixture and blend with a fork into a dough. Place on a lightly floured surface and knead gently. Leave in a cool place to rest for 15 minutes before rolling with a floured rolling pin. Cut into strips about 4 in (102 mm) long by ¼ in (7 mm) wide. Grease a baking tray and bake in a hot oven (400°F, 200°C, gas mark 6) for 10-15 minutes. Allow to cool on a wire tray before putting on serving dishes or storing in an airtight tin.

(Makes about 100 straws)

Crispy Cheese Squares

3 oz (75 g) butter
1 egg (separated)
4 oz (100 g) grated cheddar cheese
¼ teaspoon salt
½ teaspoon mustard powder
¼ teaspoon paprika
1 oz plain crisps, crushed
6 slices white bread

Cream the butter and stir in the egg yolk, grated cheese, crushed crisps and seasoning. Beat the egg white, and fold in the cheese mixture. Cut the crusts off the bread and spread thickly with the cheese mixture. Lay the bread on a greased baking tray and refrigerate for several hours. Bake in a medium oven (375°F, 190°C, gas mark 5) for 10-15 minutes until the topping is golden brown. Cut into small squares and serve while still hot.

Whether you are serving cocktails, or gin and tonic, or campari and soda, remember that any drink which calls for a slice of lemon or orange is made extra refreshing by the addition of a frozen slice of the fruit. Well in advance, slice the lemons and oranges. Open-freeze them in a freezer or the ice compartment of a refrigerator, then store them in a plastic bag in the freezer ready for use.

Don't Start Without Me

Theatre critics who attended the opening night of Joyce Rayburn's comedy *Don't Start Without Me* at the Garrick Theatre on 10 February 1971 enjoyed themselves enormously. They hated the play, but it gave them a chance to sit in the stalls sharpening their pencils and their prose in preparation for some very scathing reviews.

The plot of *Don't Start Without Me* concerns two young couples living in flats at the same North London house. Eric and Vivien (Paul Daneman and Jan Waters) live together in apparent unwedded bliss until Norman and Ruth (Brian Cox and Lucy Fleming) return from their Tenerife honeymoon, complete with suntans and sombreros. Vivien begins to hanker after similar matrimonial security, and ensuing arguments lead to temporary separations for both couples. The girls share the upstairs flat with the men living below.

Audiences liked the play. They laughed a lot at the jokes and the situation contrived by Miss Rayburn, author of the successful comedy *The Man Most Likely To. . . ,* and the survival of the play at the Garrick from February to September proved the truth of Felix Barker's statement in his Evening News review:

'If this is what the Ordinary Playgoer wants, the best thing the Professional Critic can do is to shut up and go away into a corner . . .'

I like starters that can be prepared or mostly prepared, well in advance, leaving only the final garnish to complete the dish before bringing it to the table. I also like to do the 'extra bits' that are really very easy but always seem popular, such as garlic, herb or anchovy bread, croûtons with soup, and melba toast with mousses or patés. Cheese straws make an interesting accompaniment to some starters, especially any that include apples, such as the Savoury Apple Starter (see p.31).

One of my favourite starters is also one of the easiest, invented in a hurry when Somebody Just Popped In. I had two chicken breasts in the fridge, with a solitary pot of natural yogurt, and wanted to add a starter to our main meal. I said It Really Isn't Any Trouble. And, amazingly, it wasn't.

Ginger Chicken

2 chicken breasts, off the bone
3 knobs of preserved ginger
1 small carton of natural yogurt
1 oz (25 g) butter
1 oz (25 g) flaked almonds
juice of a lemon
pinch of salt
generous grinding of black pepper
lettuce or watercress

Melt the butter gently in a small pan. Place the chicken breasts on enough silver foil to make a generous wrapping, and brush them with the butter. Season with a little salt and black pepper. Close the foil parcel leaving space around the chicken and roast in a medium oven (375°F, 190°C, gas mark 5) for 20 minutes. Slice the knobs of ginger, and mix the yogurt, ginger syrup and lemon juice together, adding the sliced ginger and most of the almonds. Season to taste. After the chicken has cooked, leave it to cool and then cut into strips. Add the strips of chicken to the yogurt sauce and leave for the flavours to develop in the fridge. To serve, put chicken mixture into individual dishes, on beds of shredded lettuce or watercress. Decorate with remaining flaked almonds, lightly grilled to make them just golden brown.

Hot Garlic Bread

1 French loaf
4 oz (100 g) butter
4 cloves garlic
pinch of salt

Remove the papery coating from the garlic and chop finely with a little salt. Mix the garlic with the butter, combining it thoroughly, using a wooden spoon. Slice the bread into individual-sized pieces, almost down to the bottom crust which is left whole. Spread the butter and garlic mixture between each slice, finishing with a little over the top of the loaf. Wrap in foil and bake in a hot oven (425°F, 220°C, gas mark 7) for 15 minutes.

For Herb Bread, mix 1 tablespoon (15 ml spoon) of mixed herbs with the butter instead of the garlic, and treat the loaf in the same way.

For Anchovy Bread, mix 1 small tin of washed, chopped anchovy fillets and half a tube of anchovy paste with the butter instead of the garlic or herbs. Then spread the butter and bake, as above.

Brian Cox, Lucy Fleming and Paul Daneman in *Don't Start Without Me*. Cartoon by Bill Hewison from 'Punch', 1971.

To make Melba Toast (named of course, after the opera singer Dame Nelly Melba), toast thick slices of white bread on both sides. Cut off the crusts. Slice horizontally through each piece, and carefully scrape off the soft breadcrumb from the underside. Cut each piece diagonally so that there are triangles of toast, and lay the pieces on a baking tray. Brown the pieces in the oven at whatever temperature is set to cook the main course, checking frequently and serving when golden brown – after about 5 minutes.

Mayonnaise

For ¼ pint (150 ml)

1 egg yolk
¼ teaspoon (¼ × 5 ml spoon) dry mustard
1 tablespoon (1 × 15 ml spoon) lemon juice

¼ pint (150 ml) olive oil or ground nut oil
1 tablespoon (1 × 15 ml spoon) boiling water
black pepper, salt

Use an egg that is at room temperature and not one that has come directly from the refrigerator. Put the yolk in a bowl with the mustard, pepper and salt and a little lemon juice. Blend well, then add the oil, drop by drop, whisking constantly. When about half the oil has been added and the mayonnaise has begun to thicken, pour in the lemon juice and the rest of the oil in a steady trickle, whisking all the time until the mixture is very thick. Whisk in the spoonful of boiling water at the last minute.

For Garlic Mayonnaise you will need 2 cloves of garlic in addition to the ingredients above. Remove the papery coating from the cloves of garlic, chop finely with a pinch of salt, and mix with the egg yolk, mustard, pepper and salt before you start to add the oil.

Cool as a Cucumber

Cool as a Cucumber was first presented on 24 March 1851 as the 'curtain-raiser' to a long evening's entertainment at the Royal Lyceum Theatre, beginning at 7pm and ending 'as near half past eleven as possible.' The main feature of the evening was the 'fairy extravaganza' *King Charming, or, The Blue Bird of Paradise*, written by the prolific author of Victorian pantomime J.R. Planché and starring the much-loved Madame Vestris in the title role. The comic afterpiece was entitled *The

Ringdoves and starred the author Charles Mathews who also appeared in Jerrold's *Cool as a Cucumber* as the rogue and imposter Horatio Plumper. Plumper was the character who caused havoc in the domestic arrangements of the Barkins household, and Jerrold wrote the farce mainly for Mathews.

Son of a comedian, the younger Charles had decided to specialise in comedy when he went on the stage in 1835:

'I had no passion for what was called the "regular drama" . . . the lighter phase of comedy, representing the more natural and less laboured school of modern life, and holding the mirror up to nature without regard to the conventionalities of the theatre, was the aim I had in view.'

Mathews married Lucy Eliza Vestris in 1838, three years after he began acting at the Olympic Theatre, which she managed. At the Olympic, at Covent Garden Theatre, and at the Lyceum (which they managed from 1847 until the death of Vestris in 1856), they made many improvements on the hitherto crude type of burlesque that was popular in contemporary theatres. They also provided elegant staging, an innovation at that time, even for light plays such as *Cool as a Cucumber*.

Since from Elizabethan times comic interludes were 'stuffed' between other acts, the word farce developed from the French word 'farcir', meaning 'to stuff'. *Cool as a Cucumber* was a farce: and so for this summer starter, a recipe for stuffed cucumber which is light and suitable before a rich main course.

Madame Vestris as King Charming.

Charles Mathews as Horatio Plumper.

Interior of the Royal Lyceum Theatre, c.1851.

Stuffed Cucumber

**1 cucumber
6 oz (175 g) cream cheese
2 tablespoons (2 × 15 ml
    spoons) soured cream
small punnet strawberries**

**juice of ½ lemon
black pepper
salt
lettuce leaves for garnish**

Cut the cucumber in half, lengthwise. Remove the seeds with the tip of a teaspoon, and discard. Cut each half cucumber into two so that you have four cucumber 'boats' for the filling. Remove the flesh from the cucumber carefully and put in a colander. Sprinkle with a little salt and leave for 1 hour to draw the juices. Rinse and pat dry with kitchen paper.

Mix the cream cheese and soured cream together with a fork, or in a blender. Put the cucumber flesh in a bowl together with the strawberries, hulled and sliced. Add the cream cheese and soured cream mixture, with lemon juice, salt and black pepper to taste. Spoon this mixture into the cucumber shells and serve on beds of lettuce leaves.

From the souvenir programme, 1900.

ROYAL STRAND THEATRE.

In the Soup

In the Soup, described in the programme as 'A New and Original Farcical Comedy in Three Acts' by Mr Ralph Lumley, was first produced at the Royal Strand Theatre on 28 August 1900. In the popular 19th-century tradition it was preceded by a curtain-raiser, a one-act comedy by a certain Mr T. Gideon Warren.

A farce 'in the French manner', *In The Soup* was particularly successful because of its more risqué elements, and it ran for 278 consecutive performances. The characters included a French ingénue who spoke her lines 'with a dainty accent', and the plot revolved around the humiliation of a wife who was obliged to prepare the food for one of her own dinner parties due to the indisposition of her cook. By mistake the soup included some sleeping draught – and, to the horror of the hostess, two couples were discovered asleep after dinner 'in compromising situations.'

The Royal Strand Theatre was situated on the site presently occupied by Aldwych underground station, near Somerset House. The theatre which the audiences of *In The Soup* visited had been rebuilt in 1882, although there had been a Strand Theatre on that site since 1831. Its name was changed several times but it became the Royal Strand in 1858, eventually being closed and demolished in 1905. The present Strand Theatre is further west, on the opposite side of the road.

The following recipe includes no sleeping draught, but the inclusion of the apple adds an intriguing flavour and prompts enquiries as to what, exactly, is 'in the soup'.

Apple, Celery and Onion Soup

This can be served hot or cold

4 sticks celery
1 lb (450 g) cooking apples
1 medium onion
2 oz (50 g) butter
1 tablespoon (1 × 15 ml spoon) curry powder

1 pint (600 ml) chicken stock
¼ pint (150 ml) single cream
black pepper
salt
paprika

Peel and core the apples and chop them into small pieces. Wash the celery. Peel the onion and chop the vegetables. Melt the butter in a frying pan. Fry the celery, onion and apple gently for 5 minutes until soft but not brown. Sprinkle the curry powder on to the vegetables and cook for a further minute. Add the chicken stock which can be made with a stock cube. Cover the pan and simmer for 30 minutes.

Liquidise the soup in a blender. Add the cream, and season to taste with pepper and salt.

Chill the soup if is is to be served cold, or heat through gently if it is to be served hot. Sprinkle it with a little paprika before serving with croûtons or melba toast.

Music sheet cover, and illustrations from 'The Sketch', 1927.

The Butter and Egg Man

With the importing of George S. Kaufman's comedy from Broadway to London, an unfamiliar Amerian slang term was also introduced to Britain. A 'butter and egg man' meant someone who was foolish with money – in this case one Peter Jones who speculates his capital on a doomed theatrical venture. Tom Douglas played the part of Jones while Frank Conlan and Robert Middlemas were the two swindling theatrical managers who enticed Jones and his money into their worthless ventures. Carol Goodner played the sympathetic secretary with whom Jones fell in love.

The Butter and Egg Man had run successfully for a year on Broadway, where Kaufman's quick-fire repartee and American humour were fully appreciated. In London after the first night at the Garrick Threatre on 30 August 1927, the critic of The Times was disdainful of its lack of character development and 'style of mechanical liveliness called "pep" by which it is given an appearance of superficial brilliance which hides many of its faults and keeps the audience in good humour.' Hard words, indeed, but the good-humoured audiences kept the play running at the Garrick until October 1927.

Kaufman, born in Pennsylvania in 1885, was one of America's most successful playwrights. He started his career as a satirical journalist and wrote *The Butter and Egg Man* on his own. Some of his best plays, however, were written in collaboration with Moss Hart, and together they wrote eight plays including *The Man Who Came to Dinner* and *Once in a Lifetime*. Kaufman appeared in the original production of *Once in a Lifetime*, the play about the start of 'talking pictures', in New York in 1930. When it was revived in London by the Royal Shakespeare Company at the Aldwych Theatre in 1979 the American humour was far more appreciated in London than it had been fifty years before. Kaufman's witty one-liners were much enjoyed – one-liners such as his comment on his own career:

'I didn't go from rags to riches, I went from Pittsburgh to Broadway, and that's further still.'

Creamy Egg Tartlets

CHEESE PASTRY
4 oz (100 g) plain flour
pinch of salt
2 oz (50 g) butter
2 tablespoons (2 × 15 ml spoons) water
juice of ½ lemon
2 oz (50 g) cheddar cheese

FILLING
3 eggs
¼ pint (150 ml) milk
1 oz (25 g) butter
black pepper
salt
parsley for garnish

To make the cheese pastry, sieve the flour with a pinch of salt into a bowl and add the butter, cut into small pieces. Rub the fat into the flour with the fingertips until the mixture resembles breadcrumbs. Grate the cheese into the bowl. Add the water and lemon juice into the centre of the mixture and blend with a fork into a dough. Place on a lightly floured surface and knead gently. Leave in a cool place to rest for 15 minutes before rolling with a floured rolling-pin. Cut the pastry into 8 rounds with a 2½ in (6 cm) pastry cutter. Lightly grease 8 tartlet tins and line with pastry. Bake blind in a hot oven (400°F, 200°C gas mark 6) for 10-15 minutes. Keep the cases warm while making the filling. Chop the parsley for the garnish.

For the filling, beat the eggs with the milk. Melt the ounce of butter in a saucepan over a low heat and cook the mixture gently, stirring constantly with a wooden spoon until the eggs are creamy and scrambled, but still slightly runny. Season to taste. Pile the mixture into the tartlet cases and sprinkle with chopped parsley. Serve immediately: 2 tartlets for each serving.

Edith Evans and Cedric Hardwicke in *The Apple Cart*. Cover from 'The Play Pictorial', 1927.

The Apple Cart

In the summer of 1929 when Londoners were flocking to see Noel Coward's new operetta *Bitter Sweet* (see p.105), the public who visited the Malvern Festival were being presented with very different fare – *The Apple Cart* – a new play by the 73 year-old George Bernard Shaw.

Shaw, who began his career as a novelist and critic, did not become a playwright until he was almost forty. A committed socialist and founder member of the Fabian Society, he liked to write to make people think, and preferred to call himself 'a thinker' rather than 'a dramatist'. He often prefaced his plays with lengthy discussions about their philosophical and political meanings, but they also often contained much wit and style. *Widower's Houses* (1892) was Shaw's earliest play, followed by others including *Candida* (1895), *The Devil's Disciple* (1897), *Major Barbara* (1905), *Pygmalion* (1913) and *Saint Joan* (1923).

Shaw's earliest plays were not performed in the commercial theatre until after the turn of the century. Several, however, were produced by The Independent Theatre, a private theatre club founded in 1891 by J.T. Grein specifically to perform plays which had 'literary and artistic rather than commercial value.' After the demise of The Independent Theatre Club in 1897 the Incorporated Stage Society presented first productions of Shaw's works. By 1929 the founder of the Malvern Festival, Sir Barry Jackson, was a great champion of Shaw works and produced ten of his plays at the festivals between 1929 and 1939.

With Cedric Hardwicke as King Magnus and Edith Evans as Orinthia in the original production of *The Apple Cart*, Shaw described the play as 'a comedy in which a King defeats an attempt by his popularly elected Prime Minister to deprive him of the right to influence public opinion through the press and platform.' In it, Shaw took a sardonic look at the future of England, mixing the fantastic and the realistic in a framework akin to 19th-century burlesque. Opening at the Malvern Festival on 19 August 1929, it transferred to the Queen's Theatre in London on 17 September 1929, where it ran successfully for 258 performances.

Many notable actors have been attracted to this play. In 1953 a revival at the Haymarket Theatre starred Margaret Leighton and Noel Coward as Orinthia and the King, while Penelope Keith and Keith Michell played the same roles in a production at the Phoenix Theatre in 1977. A recent revival at the Haymarket Theatre in February 1986 featured Peter O'Toole and Susannah York with a distinguished cast which included Michael Denison, Marius Goring, Bernard Braden, Dora Bryan and Moira Lister.

Savoury Apple Starter

4 dessert apples
2 sticks celery
2 oz (50 g) cheddar cheese
2 oz (50 g) walnuts
¼ pint (150 ml) soured cream
juice of ½ lemon
black pepper
salt

Wash the apples and slice a thin piece from the bottom of each, so that they stand upright. Cut a lid from the top of each apple, and put the lid aside. With a teaspoon carefully remove the flesh from the inside of the apples, without piercing the skin. Remove the pips and cores, and discard. Dice the apple flesh and place in a bowl, squeezing the lemon juice on the flesh to prevent the apple discolouring.

Wash and chop the celery. Dice the cheese and chop the walnuts; add with the soured cream to the apple flesh. Season to taste and pile the mixture back into the apple shells, replacing their lids. Serve with cheese straws made from cheese pastry recipe (p.29)

GARRICK

THEATRE — CHARING CROSS ROAD, W.C.2. — TELEPHONE TEMple BAR 4601

LESSEES: PENROSE SCENIC STUDIOS LTD.   LICENSED BY THE LORD CHAMBERLAIN TO GILBERT BROWN

MONDAY to THURSDAY at 8 p.m.   **FRIDAY and SATURDAY (Two Performances) at 6.0 and 8.30**

BY ARRANGEMENT WITH JOHN FORBES-SEMPILL LTD.

MICHAEL CODRON
IN ASSOCIATION WITH
EDWARD KASSNER
PRESENTS

share my lettuce

A DIVERSION WITH MUSIC

WITH

Philip Gilbert
by kind permission of the J. Arthur Rank Organisation

Maggie Smith

Roderick Cook

Barbara Evans

Johnny Greenland

Kenneth Mason

Heather Linson
and
Kenneth Williams

WRITTEN BY
Bamber Gascoigne

MUSIC COMPOSED BY
Keith Statham and
Patrick Gowers

DESIGNED BY
Disley Jones

DIRECTED BY
Eleanor Fazan

"A CHAMPAGNE BUBBLE OF A SHOW"
—JOHN BARBER, DAILY EXPRESS

A. E. KING LTD., LONDON, W.13. EAL. 7029

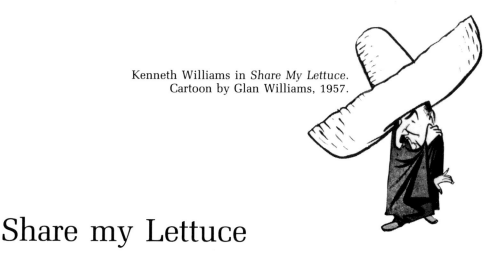

Kenneth Williams in *Share My Lettuce*.
Cartoon by Glan Williams, 1957.

Share my Lettuce

Princess Margaret was much amused by the revue *Share My Lettuce*. Visiting the show with the Queen Mother a month after it opened at the Comedy Theatre on 25 September 1957, her attempts to stifle her giggles with a handkerchief were gleefully noted in the newspapers. The revue had transferred to the West End from the Lyric Theatre in Hammersmith – the author a 22 year-old Cambridge undergraduate called Bamber Gascoigne, being described by one reviewer as 'a man with plenty to say in the future, and the wit to say it.'

With musical arrangements by Keith Statham and Patrick Gowers, the revue included dances choreographed by Eleanor Fazan and sketches on subjects ranging from cocktail parties to tube travel. Described in the programme as 'a Diversion with Music', the final sketch before the interval involved the cast in filling the stage with bubbles.

Two of the actors particularly singled out for praise in *Share My Lettuce* were Maggie Smith and Kenneth Williams. For Maggie Smith this was her first appearance on the London stage, though she had already acted in Oxford and starred on Broadway. Kenneth Williams, described in reviews as 'a magnificently assured performer', was praised for his superb facial expressions and vocal range, and was compared favourably to the great comedienne Beatrice Lillie. Assured performer that he undoubtedly is, Mr Williams was still unfortunate enough to experience an actor's nightmare later in the run. On the afternoon of 23 October he awoke from a 'brief rest' half an hour after the matinée was due to begin. Since his understudy was ill, the performance was cancelled and the popular lettuce was not shared that afternoon!

Reflecting on *Share My Lettuce*, Bamber Gascoigne recently recalled:

'I have spent much of my life regretting our title, because people always come up to me and say "Did so enjoy that revue of yours, what was it called – *Salad Days*?" So how pleasant to discover, thirty years later, that it has provided a passport into this splendid gathering. And higher up the menu than Julian Slade!

Lettuce Soup

Cartoon by Glan Williams, 1957.

This can be served hot or cold.

1 large lettuce
1 medium onion
1 small potato
2 oz (50 g) butter
¾ pint (450 ml) chicken stock
¼ pint (150 ml) milk
¼ teaspoon (¼ × 5 ml spoon) ground nutmeg
¼ pint (150 ml) single cream
black pepper
salt

Wash and shred the lettuce. Peel and chop the onion finely. Peel and chop the potato into small chunks. Melt the butter in a frying pan. Fry the onion, potato and lettuce gently for 10 minutes. Add the chicken stock, which can be made with a stock cube, milk and nutmeg. Cover the pan and simmer for 30 minutes.

Liquidise the soup in a blender. Add the cream, and season to taste with pepper and salt. Chill the soup if it is to be served cold, or heat through gently if it is to be served hot. Serve with croûtons or melba toast.

Barbara Evans, Kenneth Williams, Maggie Smith, Kenneth Mason and Phillipa Gilbert in 'Bubble Man' from *Share My Lettuce*. From 'The Sketch', 1957.

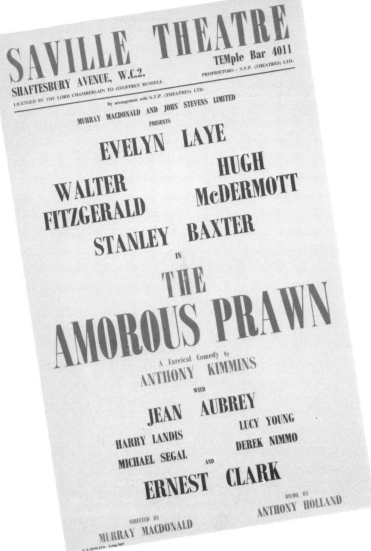

The Amorous Prawn

Opening at the Saville Theatre on 9 December 1959, Anthony Kimmins' farce *The Amorous Prawn* achieved the admirable feat of starring the beautiful Evelyn Laye and introducing to the London stage the young comedian Stanley Baxter. With a cast which included Hugh McDermott, Ernest Clark and Derek Nimmo, the show could hardly fail, though The Observer critic noted rather pompously the following morning:

Those who are allergic to stage Americans, stock military jokes and clean fun, ought to stay away. Less demanding theatregoers will enjoy themselves a lot... and recommend it to friends with healthy extrovert children to entertain.'

The play is set in a stately Scottish mansion, comandeered by the War Office as a military headquarters. When the General Officer Commanding leaves on a Pacific Mission his wife (Evelyn Laye), transforms the residence into a guest house and persuades Corporal Green (Stanley Baxter), to become the hotel manager. Wealthy Americans, played by Hugh McDermott and Michael Segal, are encouraged to stay at the hotel, lured by promises of salmon fishing at the bottom of the garden. The scheme is ruined by the unexpected arrival of the General, and the visit of an enigmatic character known only as 'The Prawn'.

A simple, farcical play with excellent actors, The Amorous Prawn opened in the West End shortly before Christmas and was a success. As the critic of The Daily Telegraph, W.A. Darlington, remarked:

'The Amorous Prawn . . . has presented theatrical London with something of which at the moment it stands in great need – a good hearty farcical comedy at which you can throw back your head and laugh without shame.'

The play transferred to the Piccadilly Theatre on 23 January 1961 and audiences went on laughing at it for a total of 911 performances.

Hugh McDermott, Ernest Clark and Evelyn Laye in The Amorous Prawn. From 'The Tatler', 1959.

Whisky Prawn Avocado

2 ripe avocados
4 oz (100 g) shelled prawns
¼ pint (150 ml) soured cream
4 tablespoons (4 × 15 ml spoons) mayonnaise
2 tablespoons (2 × 15 ml spoons) whisky
black pepper
salt
lettuce leaves for garnish

If you are using frozen prawns, defrost them and pat them dry with kitchen paper to remove excess moisture. Put them in a bowl with the soured cream, mayonnaise and whisky. Mix together thoroughly and season to taste. Halve the avocados, remove the stones and spoon the filling into the centre of each avocado. Serve on beds of lettuce leaves.

Bonne Soupe

Félicien Marceau's comedy *Bonne Soupe*, which had been a success in Paris, opened in London at the Comedy Theatre on 23 October 1961. The English version, a translation by Kitty Black, starred Coral Browne, Erica Rogers, Nigel Davenport and Peter Illing. The play told the story of Marie-Paule's life, related by Marie-Paule herself as she wryly looked back on the past 20 years – her early seduction; her days as a mistress; her success as the proprietor of a bar in the Champs-Elysées, and her comfortable married life as the respectable wife of a rich industrialist.

Coral Browne played Marie-Paule the commentator, always on stage, smartly dressed in a black Balmain dress, while scenes from her past were acted episodically in front of her. Erica Rogers played the young Marie-Paule dressed in a weary orange dress, from time to time exchanging comments with her narrator. Peter Bowles was among the actors who contributed to the humorous delineation of the men in Marie-Paule's life, and the sets on which the scenes were acted were designed by Disley Jones. The director was Eleanor Fazan, who had choreographed and directed *Share My Lettuce* four years previously at the same theatre, working with the same designer.

Coral Browne and Erica Rogers in *Bonne Soupe*.
Cartoon by Bill Hewison from 'Punch', 1961.

Critics disagreed with each other about *Bonne Soupe*. Some, like The Guardian critic, found it 'a very thin soup', but Harold Hobson enjoyed it enormously, because it was entertaining, laughable and frank: 'an excellent though unedifying entertainment, very funny, subtler than it seems and perfectly directed.' As he wrote: 'Better, any day, in the theatre, a live tart than a dead saint.' Audiences agreed with Hobson and the play's run continued at Wyndham's Theatre, where it transferred on 13 February 1962, achieving a total run of 286 performances.

Carrot and Yogurt Soup

1 lb (450 g) carrots
1 medium onion
1 clove garlic
2 oz (50) butter
1 tablespoon (1 × 15 ml spoon) dry sherry
1 pint (600 ml) beef stock
¼ pint (150 ml) natural yogurt
black pepper
salt

Peel and chop the carrots. Peel and chop the onion. Remove the papery coating from the clove of garlic and chop it finely with a little salt. Melt the butter in a frying pan. Fry the carrots, onion and garlic gently for 5 minutes until soft but not brown. Add the beef stock, which can be made with a stock cube. Cover the pan and simmer for 30 minutes.

Liquidise the soup in a blender. Add the sherry and yogurt, and season to taste. Reheat gently and serve.

Theatre Royal, Hay Market.

✱✱✱ *The New Operatic Comedy, call'd "Sweethearts and Wives," still encreasing in popularity on each representation, will be repeated This Evening, and on Friday next.*

This Evening, WEDNESDAY, August 27, 1828,
Will be perform'd (for the thirty third time) in Three Acts,
A New Operatic Comedy, call'd

Sweethearts and Wives.

With NEW MUSIC, SCENES, and DRESSES.
The MUSIC Composed and Selected by Messrs. WHITAKER, NATHAN, T. COOKE, and PERRY.

The Principal Characters by
Mr. TERRY.   Mr. VINING.
Mr. DAVIS.   Mr. WILLIAMS.
Mr. LISTON.
Miss LOVE.
Miss CHESTER.
Mrs. C. JONES.   Mrs. GARRICK.

After which (8th time this Season) the Comic Piece of

MATCH - MAKING.

Mr. Matchem, Mr. TERRY.
Col. Rakeley, Mr. VINING.   Capt. Belmont, Mr. JOHNSON.
Shuffle, Mr. HARLEY.
Servant, Mr. C. JONES.
Lady Emily, Mrs. CHATTERLEY.

To conclude with (acted but once) a New Farce, in Two Acts, with Songs, call'd

"Fish out of Water."

The MUSIC Composed by Mr. PERRY.
Sam Savoury, Mr. LISTON.
Sir George Courtley, Mr. POPE.
Alderman Gayfare, Mr. YOUNGER.
Charles Gayfare, Mr. VINING.
Steward, Mr. WILLIAMS.   Footman, Mr. WYNNE.
Ellen Courtley, Miss LOVE.
Lucy, Mrs. C. JONES.

BOXES 5s.   PIT 3s.   FIRST GALLERY 2s.   SECOND GALLERY 1s.
The Doors to be Opened at Six o'Clock, and the Performances to begin at Seven.
Places for the Boxes to be taken of Mr. Massingham, at the Theatre, Daily, from Ten till Five o'Clock.
N. B. PRIVATE BOXES may be had, nightly, by application at the Box-Office.
Vivat Rex !

✱✝✱ The New Farce produced last Night, under the Title of

"FISH OUT OF WATER,"

having been honoured with decided and most brilliant approbation throughout, will be repeated Every Evening till further Notice.

TO-MORROW, TWELVE PRECISELY. After which, The HIGHLAND REEL.
Mc. Gilpin, Mr. Williams, Sandy, Mr. Leoni Lee, Shelty, Mr. Liston, Charley, Mr. W. West, Capt. Dash, Mr. Coveney, Serjeant Jack, Mr. Tayleure, Laird of Ransey, Mr. Lee, Croudy, Mr. Hammond, Jenny, Miss Paton, Moggy, Miss Love. To conclude with FISH OUT OF WATER.
On FRIDAY, SWEETHEARTS AND WIVES. With FISH OUT OF WATER.
On SATURDAY, The YOUNG QUAKER, with FISH OUT OF WATER.

Printed by T. Woodfall, Little Queen St. Westminster.

HAY MARKET. THEATRE.

Fish out of Water

Joseph Lunn's farce *Fish out of Water* was originally presented as a comic afterpiece at the Theatre Royal, Haymarket, on 26 August 1823. The evening's entertainment comprised three plays, two of them starring the popular comedian John Liston. In review of the performance on 27 August a critic noted:

'The numerous audience enjoyed the humours of the new farce of *Fish out of Water* which on this its second performance was received with unmixed applause. The scene where Sam Savoury is compelled to sit down and write the letter before the Ambassador is highly laughable from the manner in which Mr Liston acts it.'

Appropriately for this book, Sam Savoury was a cook who in the play is mistaken as the applicant for the post of secretary in the house of a gentleman; the applicant was, naturally enough, mistaken for the cook. The play was later revived at the Olympic Theatre entitled *The Cook and the Secretary*.

John Liston (1776-1846), had begun his acting career in 1799 when he made his first professional stage appearance at the Haymarket Theatre in *The Iron Chest*, and after six years on the provincial circuits, he returned to the Haymarket for the summer season of 1805. This was the beginning of his 25-year association with the Haymarket, and by 1823 he was the highest paid comedian on the London stage. His talent for comedy was remarkable – as one contemporary noted:

'He must be seen to be comprehended. Other actors labour to be comic. I see nothing like labour in Liston.'

Derby factory figure of John Liston as Paul Pry, c.1830.

Perhaps Liston's greatest success was as the interfering busybody Paul Pry in the play of the same name which he first performed at the Haymarket Theatre in September 1825. Madame Vestris played the maid Phoebe who sang 'Cherry Ripe', and the play ran for an unprecedented 114 performances. Liston's character with his catchphrase 'Just dropped in. I hope I don't intrude' inspired numerous engravings and paintings, figurines and toby jugs.

When *Fish out of Water* was presented at the Haymarket in 1823 the theatre boasted the same Corinthian pillared exterior that we know today. It was the second Theatre Royal in the Haymarket, designed by John Nash and opened in 1821. The first Theatre Royal was situated slightly to the north of its present site and had opened in 1720, being granted a Royal Patent in 1766 to present summer seasons of plays during the annual closure of Drury Lane and Covent Garden Theatres.

Baked Salmon Trout with Apple, Cashew and Mint Stuffing

1 large salmon trout (2-2 lbs) (1 kg-1.5 kg), cleaned but left whole	STUFFING
	1 oz (25 g) butter
	1 lb (100 g) onions
1 oz (25 g) butter	1 lb (100 g) cooking apples
salt	2 oz (50 g) shelled cashew nuts (not salted)
black pepper	
1 lemon	6 mint leaves, chopped
	salt
	black pepper

To make the stuffing, peel and finely chop the onions and the cored apples. Melt 1 oz (25 g) butter over a low heat in a frying pan. Cook the onions until softened and add the apples, chopped cashew nuts, and mint leaves. Season with salt and black pepper and fry gently, stirrring occasionally, for a further five minutes.

Grease a large piece of baking foil with 1 oz (25 g) butter and lay the fish on the foil. Season lightly with salt and black pepper. Open the fish, and fill it with as much stuffing mixture as possible. Spoon the remaining stuffing over the fish. Fold the edges and ends of the baking foil to make a loose parcel, enclosing the fish completely. Place on a large baking tray or roasting tin and bake in a medium oven (350°F, 180°C, gas mark 4) for twenty minutes per 1 lb (450 g).

When cooked, unwrap the fish. Spoon the stuffing mixture that covered the fish into a bowl and put it back in the oven to keep warm. Lift the skin from the fish and separate the flesh down the centre along the line of the bone. Gently slice the fish into servings, lifting the bone away. To each serving add some stuffing from inside the fish and extra stuffing from the bowl. Add a wedge of lemon to each serving.

Note: A large salmon trout will serve six, and a smaller one four.

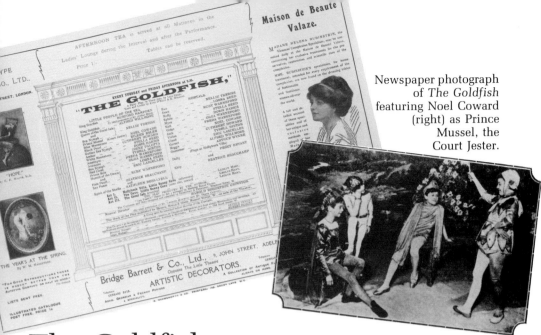

Newspaper photograph of *The Goldfish* featuring Noel Coward (right) as Prince Mussel, the Court Jester.

The Goldfish

On 27 January 1911 at the Little Theatre a 12-year old boy made his first appearance on the London stage in a musical play for children, *The Goldfish*. Reggie and King Goldfish were played by another 12 year-old, Alfred Willmore, who later changed his name to Micheál MacLiammóir. The precocious boy playing Jack and Prince Mussel was called Noel Coward. His mother had answered an advertisement in 'The Daily Mirror' which read: 'Handsome attractive boy wanted for a part in Christmas pantomime. Must be talented'. After singing and dancing for the author, Lila Field, in a rehearsal room near Baker Street, Noel Coward was given the part. *The Goldfish* ran at the Little Theatre for a week of matinées; was succeeded by two revivals at the Royal Court in April, and produced at the Crystal Palace for two matinées in May. Coward wrote later that he could not remember the house in which he was born, but that he certainly could remember:

'The theatre where I was born and the play in which I was born and that play is *The Goldfish* which retains for one rapidly ageing little boy a magic that will never die.'

Coward's love of the theatre began at an early age. As he said:

'On my fifth birthday my mother injected the "musical comedy" virus into my bloodstream by taking me to see *The Dairymaids* at the Grand Theatre, Croydon.'

Delighted and bewildered by the cavorting ladies, Noel was taken to more musical plays by his adoring mother, and he became entranced by Gertie Millar, the Gaiety girl whom Coward called: 'the epitome of what a musical comedy star should be.'

Two years after appearing in *The Goldfish*, the promising young actor was chosen to appear in *Hannelle* at the Liverpool Playhouse. Leaving home for the first time was a momentous experience, and Coward later remembered meeting some of the cast on the train, particularly 'a vivacious little girl with ringlets.' This 14 year-old girl was Gertrude Lawrence, who grew up to star with Coward in plays and musical comedies by him including *Private Lives* and *Tonight At 8.30* (see p.72).

Smoked Haddock Pie

1½ lbs (675 g) smoked haddock
½ pint (300 ml) milk
¼ pint (150 ml) water
1 oz (25 g) butter
1 bay leaf
1 lb (450 g) onions
1 lb (450 g) potatoes
¼ lb (100 g) mushrooms
2 eggs
2 oz (50 g) cheddar cheese
black pepper
salt

SAUCE
1 pint (600 ml) fish stock
2 oz (50 g) butter
2 oz (50 g) plain flour
black pepper
salt

Poach the smoked haddock in the milk and water with the bay leaf for about 15 minutes, until the fish is tender. Strain off the liquid and reserve for the sauce. Discard the bayleaf. Remove the skin and flake the fish. Peel and slice the onions. Melt 1 oz (25 g) butter in a frying pan and gently fry the onions for 5 minutes until soft. Wipe and chop the mushrooms and add to the onions, cooking for a further 3 minutes. Hardboil the eggs. Plunge them into cold water. Peel and slice. Peel and slice the potatoes and cook in boiling salted water for about 5 minutes, until just soft.

Make a white sauce by melting 2 oz (50 g) butter in a saucepan, mixing 2 oz (50 g) plain flour into the butter and cooking gently for 1 minute. Add the fish stock gradually, mixing well and cooking until the sauce is smooth and thick. Stir constantly with a wooden spoon. Season to taste.

Lightly butter an ovenproof casserole dish and layer the potatoes, fish, sliced egg, onion, mushrooms and sauce, ending with a layer of potatoes and more sauce. Grate the cheese on the top and dot with butter. Cook in medium oven (375°F, 190°C, gas mark 5) for 30 minutes. Finish browning the topping under a hot grill before serving.

Suggested wine: Pouilly-Fumé (Loire), or Pouilly Blanc-Fumé (California).

GLYNDEBOURNE

Lessees: GLYNDEBOURNE SOCIETY LTD.

Artistic Director: Carl Ebert   Director and General Manager: Rudolf Bing

---

FIRST NIGHT, FRIDAY, JUNE 20th, 1947

THE ENGLISH OPERA GROUP LTD.

WHO COME AS VISITORS TO GLYNDEBOURNE, PRESENT

in association with THE ARTS COUNCIL OF GREAT BRITAIN

ALBERT HERRING

A Comic Opera in Three Acts

Music by	Libretto by	Designed by
BENJAMIN BRITTEN	ERIC CROZIER	JOHN PIPER

Conductor:	Producer:
BENJAMIN BRITTEN	FREDERICK ASHTON

Lady Billows an elderly autocrat	JOAN CROSS
Florence her housekeeper	GLADYS PARR
Miss Wordsworth Head Teacher at the School	MARGARET RITCHIE
Mr. Gedge the Vicar	WILLIAM PARSONS
Mr. Upfold the Mayor	ROY ASHTON
Superintendent Budd	NORMAN LUMSDEN
Sid butcher's shophand	FREDERICK SHARP
Albert Herring from the greengrocer's	PETER PEARS
Nancy from the bakery	NANCY EVANS
Mrs. Herring Albert's mother	BETSY DE LA PORTE
Emmie ⎫	LESLIE DUFF
Cis ⎬ tiresome village children	ANNE SHARP
Harry ⎭	DAVID SPENSER

The scene is Loxford, a small market town in East Suffolk, in the year 1900

ACT ONE (April)—SCENE I: The morning room of Lady Billows' house.
Interlude: The Village Children.
SCENE II: Mrs. Herring's greengrocer's shop.

ACT TWO (May Day)—SCENE I: A marquee in the Rectory garden.
Interlude: May Day Feast and Nocturne.
SCENE II: The greengrocer's shop.

ACT THREE (May the Second)—The greengrocer's shop.

Dinner Interval after Act One.

Albert Herring

Albert Herring, a comic opera in three acts, with music by Benjamin Britten and libretto by Eric Crozier, was first performed at Glyndebourne on 20 June 1947. It was conducted by Britten and produced by Frederick Ashton, with scenery and costumes designed by John Piper.

Eric Crozier described how the idea for the opera came about:

'Albert Herring was conceived in October 1946. We needed a new opera to launch the first independent season of the English Opera Group, in summer 1947. It should be a companion and contrast to *The Rape of Lucretia*, suitable for a performance by a small company of singers and twelve soloist musicians.

It was Crozier's idea to make a comic opera based on Maupassant's short story *Madame Husson's Rose King*, which would only need simple sets and a small cast, ideal for an opera to take on tour. Britten asked Crozier to write the libretto, transferring the action from Maupassant's Normandy to Britten's beloved Suffolk. Working together, Britten and Crozier drew up a list of characters and voices, and Crozier established at which points Britten would like to use various musical forms. Crozier then started to write the libretto. As he said: 'Being neither poet nor playwright I set about my first draft with many misgivings and only three determinations – to be simple, to be sensible, and to be singable.'

The action is set in the imaginary Suffolk village of Loxford in April and May 1900, when the villagers are preparing for their May Festival. Since no suitably pure girls are available to be the May Queen, Albert Herring is chosen to be King of the May. Lady Billows sings:

'May King! May King!
  Remarkable position
Cause a great sensation
  On the First of May.'

Peter Pears played Albert Herring, with Betsy de la Porte as his mother and Joan Cross as the dictatorial Lady Billows. After Albert's Coronation he leaves his mother's greengrocer's shop armed with his £25 prize money, determined to try 'a taste of certain things/The Prayer Book catalogues amongst its sins.' The villagers mourn him, fearing his early death, whereupon he returns, thoroughly unrepentant and grateful for escaping from his mother's apron strings at last.

Peter Pears as Albert Herring with Joan Cross as Lady Billows and William Parsons as the Vicar in *Albert Herring*, Glyndebourne 1947.

Stuffed Herring with Caper Sauce

4 large herrings (boned and gutted)
2 oz (50 g) mushrooms
1 large onion
1 tablespoon (1 × 15 ml spoon) capers
2 oz (50 g) fresh white breadcrumbs
1 oz (25 g) butter
1 lemon
sprig of parsley
black pepper
salt

SAUCE
½ pint (300 ml) milk
1 oz (25 g) butter
1 oz (25 g) plain flour
1 tablespoon (1 × 15 ml spoon) caper juice
1 tablespoon (1 × 15 ml spoon) capers
black pepper
salt

Wash the herrings and pat them dry. Melt 1 oz (25 g) butter in a frying pan. Peel and chop the onion finely. Wipe and chop the mushrooms. Fry the onions gently in the butter until soft for about 3 minutes and add the mushrooms for a further 2 minutes. Season with pepper and salt. In a bowl mix the breadcrumbs with 1 tablespoon (1 × 15 ml spoon) capers and the juice of half the lemon. Add the mushroom and onion mixture and a little chopped parsley. Open each fish. Stuff them with a quarter of the filling mixture and fold them back into a fish shape. Lay them on lightly buttered aluminium cooking foil and seal the foil around the fish. Place on a baking tray and cook in a moderate oven (350°F, 180°C, gas mark 4) for 45 minutes. Cut the remaining half-lemon into four wedges, and serve the fish with a garnish of parsley and lemon.

For the sauce, melt 1 oz (25 g) butter in a saucepan. Mix 1 oz (25 g) of plain flour into the butter and cook gently for 1 minute. Add the milk and the caper juice gradually, mixing well and cooking until the sauce is smooth and thick. Stir constantly with a wooden spoon. Chop the capers finely and add them to the sauce, with seasoning, just before serving. Serve sauce in a separate sauce boat.

Suggested wine: Muscat d'Alsace, or Gewurztraminer (Alsace).

Big Fish, Little Fish, Duke of York's Theatre, 1962.

Big Fish, Little Fish

Big Fish Little Fish, a 'serious comedy', by the American dramatist Hugh Wheeler, was first produced at the Duke of York's Theatre on 18 September 1962. The setting was a fairly shabby but comfortable New York bachelor flat with a suitably untidy kitchen, and the designer, Jac Vicenza had created an impressive backcloth depicting towering skyscrapers to emphasise the location.

The plot concerned William Baker, once a celebrated academic biologist, who for the previous 20 years had been stuck in a pleasant but unchallenging rut as a publisher's assistant. The play hinges on the chance that presents itself to Baker to change his life, leave his job, mistress and friends, and to start anew in Europe. He has to decide whether his acquaintances over the past 20 years have been true friends or only parasites, and his mistress is also given cause to reflect on their relationship: '... it wasn't really love ... just sex and friendship; for all those years, just sex and friendship.'

Edith was played by Jessica Tandy, returning to the London stage for the first time since she left to live in the USA in 1940. The rôle of her husband 'suffering from ingrowing friendship' was taken by her Canadian husband, Hume Cronyn. Thomas Coley played the central character, Baker, with Frank Pettingell as another so-called friend, resembling 'a large and touchy seal'!

Critical reaction to *Big Fish Little Fish* was varied. Philip Hope-Wallace of The Guardian found it an entertaining evening, if not an artistic success, while Bernard Levin, then drama critic of the Daily Mail, could only praise Act II. Most reviewers agreed, however, that the strength of the play lay not in the plot but in the author's gift for truthful observation and witty, natural dialogue:

'... so good indeed that sometimes it sounds like conversation overheard rather than invented.'

BIG FISH Little Fish

by

HUGH WHEELER

Creamy Sole with Prawns

4 sole fillets
8 oz (225 g) shelled prawns
8 shallots
4 oz (100 g) mushrooms
¼ pint (150 ml) white wine
1 bayleaf
sprig of parsley
1 tablespoon (1 × 15 ml spoon) lemon juice

CREAMED POTATOES
2 lbs (1 kg) potatoes
2 oz (50 g) butter
¼ pint (150 ml) milk
black pepper
salt

SAUCE
1 oz (25 g) butter
1 oz (25 g) plain flour
¼ pint (150 ml) milk
¼ pint (150 ml) double cream
black pepper
salt

Wash the fillets of sole and pat them dry with kitchen paper. Wipe and slice the mushrooms and peel the shallots. Put the fish in a lightly greased ovenproof dish covered with the mushrooms, shallots, bay leaf and parsley. Season with pepper, salt and lemon juice. Add the wine and just enough water to cover the fish. Cook in medium oven (350°F, 180°C, gas mark 4) for 15 minutes. Remove the fish; carefully peel off and discard the skin together with the parsley and bayleaf. Strain off the fish liquid, reserving it for the sauce. Put the vegetables aside. While the fish is cooking, peel and boil the potatoes in lightly salted water until soft. Drain and mash them with 2 oz (50 g) butter and ¼ pint (150 ml) milk, until really creamy and smooth. Season with salt and pepper. For the sauce melt 1 oz (25 g) butter in a saucepan, mixing 1 oz (25 g) plain flour into the butter and cooking gently for 1 minute. Add the strained fish liquid and the milk gradually, mixing well and cooking until the sauce is smooth and thick. Add the cream and the prawns; if the prawns are frozen they should be defrosted and patted dry. Check the seasoning.

Arrange the creamed potato in a lightly greased ovenproof casserole, leaving the centre free for the fish. Place the fillets of sole, mushrooms and shallots in the centre and pour the cream and prawn sauce over them. Cover and heat through in a medium oven (350°F, 180°C, gas mark 4) for half an hour until the sauce is bubbling. Remove the cover from the casserole and cook for another 5 minutes until the potato is golden.

Suggested wine: A white Burgundy, e.g. Macon.

Theatre Royal, Covent Garden,

This present MONDAY, December 29, 1806,
Will be acted (first time this season) a Tragedy, called

GEORGE BARNWELL;

Or, The LONDON MERCHANT.

Thoroughgood by Mr. MURRAY, Uncle by Mr. DAVENPORT,
George Barnwell by Mr. C. KEMBLE,
Trueman by Mr. CLAREMONT, Blunt by Mr. BEVERLY,
Jailer by Mr. ABBOT, John by Mr. W. Murray, Robert by Mr. Sarjant,
Officers, Mess. Brown, Platt, Powers,
Maria by Miss BRUNTON,
Millwood by Miss SMITH,
(Being her first appearance in that character.)
Lucy by Mrs. MATTOCKS.

To which will be added, for the first time, a new Pantomime, which has been long in preparation, called

Harlequin and Mother Goose;

OR, The GOLDEN EGG.

The Scenes, Musick, Machinery, Dresses and Decorations are entirely new.
The Overture and Musick composed by Mr. Ware.
The Pantomime produced under the Direction of Mr. FARLEY—The Dances by Mr. BOLOGNA, Jun.
The SCENERY by Mess. Phillips, Whitmore, Hollogan, Grieve, Hodgings, and their Assistants.

Principal Characters.
Mother Goose, Mr. SIMMONS,
Colin, afterwards Harlequin, by Mr. KING and Mr. BOLOGNA, Jun.
Avaro, afterwards Pantaloon, Mr. L. BOLOGNA,
'Squire Bugle, afterwards Clown, Mr. GRIMALDI,
Beadle, Mr. Denman, Woodcutter, Mr. Truman,
Landlord, Mr. Bologna, Sergeant, Mr. Banks
Cabin-boy (with a Song) Master SMALLEY,
Waiters, Mess. Baker & Griffiths
Gardeners, Mess. Davis, Dick, Morelli,
Oddfish, Mr. MENAGE,
Villagers, &c. by Mess. Abbot, T. Blanchard, Brown, Burden, Everard, Fairbrother, Fairclough
Goodwin, Lee, Linton, Meyers, Monk, Odwell, W. Murray, Platt, Powers,
Reeves, Rimsdyck, Sarjant, Street, Tett, J. Tett, Thomas, Wilde.
Fairies, Masters Benton, Goodwin, Morelli, Searle,
Columbine, Miss SEARLE,
Woodcutter's Wife, Mrs WHITMORE.
Villagers, Fairies, &c. Mesdames Benton, Bologna, L. Bologna, Bristow, Cox, Cranfield, Findlay, Follett
Grimaldi, Iliff, Lefevre, Masters, Price, Slader, Watts.

In the course of the Pantomime (among others) the following NEW SCENERY will be introduced:

VILLAGE, with STORM and SUN RISE.	Hollogan	FLOWER GARDEN. — Grieve
MOTHER GOOSE'S HABITATION.	Phillips	St. DUNSTAN's CHURCH — Whitmore
HALL in AVARO's HOUSE.	Hollogan	Entrance of VAUXHALL GARDENS. — Whitmore
COUNTRY INN.	Phillips	Interior of Ditto. — Hollogan
INSIDE of Ditto.	Phillips	GROCER's SHOP, Outside. — Phillips
MARKET TOWN	Phillips	GROCER's PARLOUR. — Whitmore
WOODCUTTER's COTTAGE.	Grieve	MERMAID's CAVE. — Hollogan
PAVILION by MOONLIGHT.	Grieve	SUB-MARINE PAVILION.

The Machinery by Mess. SLOPER, BOLOGNA, Jun. CRESWELL, and GOOSTREE.
The Dresses by Mr. DICK and Mrs EGAN.

Books of the Songs to be had in the Theatre, Price 9d. No money to be returned.
Printed by ..... 2, Bow-street. Vivant Rex & Regina.

Tomorrow (11th time) the new Play of A MOTHER's VENGEANCE.
ADRIAN and ORRILA; or, The ENCHANTED ISLAND, will be on Wednesday.
The ninth night of The TEMPEST; or, the ENCHANTED ISLAND, will be on Wednesday.

Mother Goose

Mother Goose laid her first golden egg on the stage of the Theatre Royal, Covent Garden, on the evening of the 20th December 1806. Her debut, received with deafening shouts and applause, was a tremendous success. She continued to draw full houses for the next 92 evenings – the rest of that season at Covent Garden. The pantomime was revived the following October and performed by the same company at the Haymarket Theatre in December 1808, after a fire at Covent Garden in September had destroyed the theatre. *Harlequin and Mother Goose, or, The Golden Egg*, made over £20,000 profit for the theatre, although the author Tom Dibdin complained bitterly that the proprietor Mr Harris never congratulated him – even when the play became 'the constant talk of the town.'

Pantomime, with its harlequinades, spectacular transformation scenes and characters descended from the Italian drama known as 'Commedia dell'Arte', was a firm favourite with 19th-century audiences. The enormous popularity of *Mother Goose* at Covent Garden was largely due to the superb clowning of Joseph Grimaldi who had made his stage debut as a dancer in the Drury Lane pantomime *Robinson Crusoe* at the tender age of three. The strenuous acrobatics performed nightly by Grimaldi forced his retirement from the stage in 1828, when he was fifty. It is the legendary clowning of Grimaldi that has given the nickname 'Joey' to all clowns who even today meet annually to take part in a service of remembrance for him. As one contemporary noted in verse, his appeal was universal:

'GRIMALDI appears, every face wears a smile
As his comical tricks he exhibits the while;
His looks are so queer, and his singing so droll,
There are none can look grave, for he pleases the whole.'

JOE GRIMALDI,

As CLOWN in the Pantomime of Mother Goose.

"Sir, I'll just trouble you with a line."

Goose with Apricot Stuffing

1 young goose, oven-ready, about 10 lbs (4½ kg)
black pepper
salt
boiling water for basting
watercress for garnish

APRICOT STUFFING
1 large onion
2 sticks celery
goose liver
6 oz (175 g) fresh white breadcrumbs
8 oz (225 g) dried apricots
1 egg
2 tablespoons (2 × 15 ml spoons) sherry
1 teaspoon (1 × 5 ml spoon) dried sage
black pepper
salt

Soak the apricots in the sherry for at least 2 hours, turning them occasionally. Drain the apricots and chop the flesh into small pieces. Reserve any sherry that has not been absorbed, for the stuffing. Cover the goose liver with cold water. Bring to the boil and simmer for about 5 minutes. Drain, and chop finely. Peel and chop the onion. Chop the celery. Melt the butter in a frying pan, add the onion and celery and fry gently for 5 minutes, until soft. Beat the egg in a bowl and add the apricots, sherry, breadcrumbs, liver, onion, sage, pepper and salt. Stuff the goose with this mixture at the neck end, (which flavours the breast well) and secure the skin underneath the bird with a skewer. Season the bird with pepper and salt and prick the skin thoroughly with a fork or skewer to allow as much fat as possible to escape during cooking. Loosely cover the goose with foil and place on a rack over a roasting tin. Place in the centre of a hot oven (400°F, 200°C, gas mark 6) for 30 minutes, then lower the temperature to 375°F, 190°C, gas mark 5, and roast for the remaining time, allowing 20 minutes per pound, and 20 minutes extra. Baste occasionally with boiling water and remove the fat when the tin gets too full. (Keep this fat as it is excellent for cooking.) For the last hour, remove the foil from the bird to allow it to brown.

Serve surrounded by a generous watercress garnish.

Suggested wine: a Californian red, such as Zinfandel.

ROYAL OLYMPIC THEATRE

Wych Street, Strand. Lessee, Mr. G. WILD. By Authority of the Lord Chamberlain

BOXES, 3s, PIT, 1s. 6d. GALLERY, 6d.
Half-price at 9 o'Clock.—Boxes, 1s. 6d. and Pit, 1s.
PRIVATE BOXES, £1, 11s. 6d. to be had at the Box-Office, & of Mssrs. ANDREWS, SAMS, MITCHELL, SEGUIN & EBERS.

The GRIMALDI SCHOOL REVIVED!
Clown, - - - Mr. JEFFERINI.
43rd Night of the Funniest Pantomime of the Lot.

The numerous Inquiries at the Box Office for the Revival of Leman Rede's

"JACK IN THE WATER,"

ORIGINALLY PRODUCED AT THIS THEATRE, induces the Manager to announce the above Successful Drama, for the First Time this Season, and put aside, for a short period, the

"LOVES OF THE DEVILS,"

"PORK CHOPS" ready at 9 o'clock, for the 1st Time.

MONDAY, Feb. 13th, 1843, and During the Week.
The Performance will commence with (First Time this Season), an Original Domestic Burletta, by the Author of the "Rake's Progress" "Sixteen-String Jack," "Life's a Lottery," &c. entitled

JACK IN THE WATER
Or, the Ladder of Life.

The Music (old as the Hills) arranged by Mr. CALCOTT.
The Dresses by Mr. NATHAN and Assistants. The Properties by Mr. FOSTER.
The SCENERY by Mr. W. R. BEVERLY, Scott, and Assistants.

Characters in Act I.

Edward Lorrington, Esq. ...(a West Indian, of large Fortune)... Mr. GREEN
Fluxmead Fragile, ...(his Child)... Mr. FITZJAMES. Didapper, ...(Head Waiter at the Angel)... Mr. ROSS.
Dick Duffey, ...(Porter at the Angel)... Mr. SEARLE. Charles Janvery, Esq.,... Mr. BRETT.
Mr. Quillets, ...(Attorney at Law)... Mr. SCOTT. Gumbydown Dab...... Mr. ROGERS.
Joe Hatch, ...(Lord High Chancellor of the Thames)... Mr. TURNOUR.
Tom Myers..... Mr. HARTLAND. Betty..... Master HILL. Lamplighter..... Mr. WALTON.
Jack in the Water,..... Mr. G. WILD.
Tom Tug ..... Mr. PHILLIPS. Pulloway Phil..... Mr. BROWN. Bosen Bill,..... Mr. JONAS.
Clara,.....(Niece to Old Quillets). Miss Arden. Jane,..... Miss PLOWMAN. Sarah,..... Miss GRANBY.
Betty,.....(Chambermaid at the Angel)..... Miss LEBATT.

Characters in Act II.

Lorrington.. Mr. GREEN. Fragile.. Mr. FITZJAMES. Joe Hatch.. Mr. TURNOUR.
Sidney Lofton, Esq. ......(a Sergeant at Law, and Cousin to Mrs. Lorrington)...... Mr. C. BAKER.
Dick Duffey,..... Mr. SEARLE. Didapper..... Mr. ROSS. Christopher..... Mr. JONAS.
Jack in the Water,..... (Suddenly transformed into a Gentleman—with new "WANTS")..... Mr. G. WILD.
Quillets,..... Mr. SCOTT. Servants, Stewards, &c., Messrs. CONWAY, BROWN, EDWARDS, &c.
Emily Lorrington, ...(Wife of Lorrington, an Heiress in her own Right)... Miss L. MELVILLE.
Clara.. Miss LEBATT. Betty.. Mrs. Hank,.. Mr. GRANBY.

(A LAPSE OF TWELVE MONTHS IS SUPPOSED TO HAVE OCCURRED.)

Characters in Act III.

Fragile..... (just returned from Paris).. Mr. FITZJAMES. Duffey,..... (still Porter at the Angel).. Mr. SEARLE.
Jack in the Water,..... (settled a la mode de Paris)..... Mr. G. W I L D.
Didapper,..... (a Dancer at a Gaming House)..... Mr. ROSS.
Joe Hatch..... Mr. TURNOUR. Robert..... Mr. PHILLIPS. Horsleydown Dick,..... Mr. ROGERS.
Lorrington,...(a Homeless Wanderer in the Great Metropolis)..... Mr. GREEN. Quillett,..... Mr. SCOTT.
Mrs. Lorrington,..... (their lonely Messengers)..... Miss L. MELVILLE.
Betty..... Miss LEBATT. Sarah..... Miss GRANBY. Jane..... Miss PLOWMAN.

Duet.- "Splashing Along," - Miss Lebatt & Mr. G. Wild.

In the course of the Burletta, the following SCENERY and EFFECTS.—Act I.

AN APARTMENT IN A PRIVATE HOTEL.

Waterloo Bridge Stairs.
W. R. BEVERLY.

ACT II.—DWELLING OF

Joe Hatch, Lord Chancellor of the River!

APARTMENT IN QUILLET'S HOUSE.
EXTERIOR OF THE "ANGEL" HOTEL.
Picture Chamber in the Mansion of Loftus. W. R. BEVERLY

ACT III.

CHARING CROSS.

Interior of the Dwelling of Miss Emily Mornington.
(Late Mrs. LORRINGTON.)

APARTMENT IN THE "ANGEL" HOTEL.
EXTERIOR OF THE "ANGEL." INTERIOR.

Drawing Room & Conservatory
In the Villa of Miss Emily Mornington.
(W. R. BEVERLY.)

After which, (for the First Time) will be served up, an Extravagant Entertainment, prepared by the Author of the "ARTFUL DODGE" under the Gastronomic Title of

"PORK CHOPS"

Garnished with a DramATTIC Scene, by Mr. W. R. BEVERLY,
And Musical Sauce, by Mr. CALCOTT.

Septimus Snooks,...........(a "Swell-man connect'd with the Press"—vulgo, a "Penny-a-liner")........ Mr. G. WILD.
With a Description of the "LIFE OF A VAGABOND."
Mr. Darkeye Dabbs.........(a Belia-vue Conserver— After many racing years, has opted it to be retire,).... Mr. SEARLE.
Phil. Piffer,......(a late "Paddington Phil," now Conductor to a Paddington Omnibus,)...... Mr. ROGERS.
and now a Follower of Darkeye Dabbs,
Miss Chippington Chubb.....(Daughter to her Mother & Heiress Apparent to the House of her Parent)...Miss HAMILTON.
In the course of the Entertainment, the following Startling Incidents.

The GARRET! The SUPPER!! The PASSAGE!!!
The Staircase!!!! The Murder!!!!! The Poisoning!!!!!!
THE ▬▬▬▬▬▬▬▬▬▬▬ !!!!!!!
THE DENOUEMENT!

The whole to conclude with, for the 43rd Time an Original Comic Pantomime, to be entitled

HARLEQUIN & OLD COCKER
Or Arithmetic Hall & the Rule of Three!

An indisputably Original, Moral, and highly instructive Pantomime, wherein prevailing Practice, Multiplies the public pleasures, Subtracts the Sting from Melancholy, Reduces the power of grief, Divides the attention of Old and Young, and by the aid of Comical Figures, Adds to the amount of innocent enjoyments, by making up with Interest, the full Sum of Laughter.

COME IN Numbers AND SEE IT Proved!

The Opening invented and penned by Mr. NELSON LEE.
The Overture & Opening Music entirely New,.. Mr. BLEWITT, Comic Portions,.. Mr. CALCOTT.
The Dresses by Mr. NATHAN, and Madame CONSTANCE.

THE SPLENDID SCENERY, by Mr. W. R. BEVERLY,
Mr. SCOTT, & Assistants. The Machinery & Scenic Transformations, by Mr. MACKINTOSH.
The Properties, Masks and Pantomimical Changes, by Mr. FOSTER.
The WHOLE PRODUCED & GOT UP UNDER THE SUPERINTENDANCE OF
Mr. G. WILD and Mr. JEFFERINI.

Practice, t'a very industrious Youth, well known & a love of business connected to YOUNG BOLOGNA
Multiplication, (a worthy Associate, with an excellent Table, and an eye to Addition for his Client Anne) M. JEFFERINI.
Pantos, by Miss BROWN, Miss PLOWMAN, Miss YATES, Mrs WILLIAMS, and Misdlle. ANGELIQUE.
Long Division, self This Bailiff, whose keen sight even seem'd to extend his vision Mr SEARLE
Short Division,   Reduction, (Gone to his own more better days) M. WILKINS. Mr. ROGERS.
Old Cocker, the Old Man who lived in the Rules, without forsaking the Brick Master of a Preparatory Academy, M. SCOTT.
    which would now have been a Commoner.
Cipher, a Gentleman, whose fortune though a good round figure (0) is dependant on his friend Unit Mr. MICKELL.
Dame Interest, (Mother of the Bank of England and Addition, an elderly Lady with great Possessions, Sporting Character) Mr. TURNOUS
    surrounded with Loan and Bulletsholerets, and Loan upon Change—
    was not Plagued her word in practice.

Miss Addition, (the Daughter) Miss WRIGHT, Figurante, Arithmetical Queen of the Fairies, at the head of numerous Misdlle MILTON.
Union, (her Fairy Prince Minister of Neo ARDEN. Proof & Answer, (her choice Attendants) Miss G. LEBATT & Miss GRANBY.

SUBTERRANEAN PALACE OF SLATES!
OR ENCHANTED SLATE MINE.

(From the Pencil of Mr. W. R. BEVERLY.)
Coming Home Unbroken. Grand School of Accounts.

Multiplication's Appearance from the Magic Slate!

The Rustian Feast. Arrival of young Practice. Subscription for them. Threat of Arrest. Long and Short Division required. Sponge Spirits requiring a Rubber. Accounts made up, and Departure of the Head of the Firm.

Mansion of Dame Interest in the Regions of Plenty
By W. R. BEVERLY.

DESCENT OF THE FAIRY, UNITSA!

The Mansion..Addition's Lament..her Love for Practice..Multiplication's Vow..his welcome to Dame Interest in the Christmas chest.
    He'll add a fortune to a knight or spouse.
Arrival of Practice..Multiplication's Sincerity discovered. Long and Short Division appear. The Arrest. The Escape. Multiplication doubled up..Interest on the carve. Subtraction carries One, and the whole sum reversing.

Interior of the Cottage of Poverty, belonging to Reduction!
MR W. R. BEVERLY.

Commutators vote ... Power! is not a Crime, but very unanimous.
  - Multiplication in vexation, Division in so half ; The Rule of Three, it pozzles me ; And Practice divides me mad"—Vale, Our Early Days.
  Addition gives over to Reduction. Unexpected Arrivals. Practice, Multiplication, Interest and Vulgar Fractions.

ARITHMETICAL HALL, or WORLD OF FIGURES.

Approach of Her Majesty's Figure Army ! "According to Cocker,"
AND **APPEARANCE of QUEEN FIGURANTHE** IN HER
TEMPLE OF FIGURES!

Petition from Multiplication...The Queen's Statement,..Weights and Measures,..Mandate of the Fairy Queen.

THE CHARM! 2 3 4 5 6 7 8 9
1 2 3 4 5 6 7 8
1 1 1 1 1 1 1 1

"Now Anticipation—be out of all evil effect, Who first completes the Sum—returns the most"
Practice = Harlequin, - Young BOLOGNA,
Multiplication, = Clown, - Mr. JEFFERINI,
Dame Interest = Pantaloon, Mr. HARTLAND,
Miss Addition, = Columbine. - Miss WRIGHT,
Proof, = Harlequina. - Miss G. LEBATT.

Old Clothes Shop—Moses & his Sons!

Shopman, Mr. Cadler. Real One at hand. Attention: Moses and his ——. Airy, Back, Comminator, Hide Scab, Turnham Green, Vauxhall Bruin, Paddington, Poplar, ——, Canonbury, Messrs Buskin and Giles, Clarke, Simeon, Tasten and Bryan, Ben-den, Mr. Rethery, Fog, Mr. Kavanagh, —— the delicacies of various corner house hondship- (I have oft Swan. Skiff and Lad with a regular Rank-er-ti-)

QUADRANT - Field. Stationer, Corner of Air Street.
Sookrane, Mr. A. J. Smiterton. ——————— In the Furnishing, ———————

THE OLD PARR'S HEAD, AND CHINA SHOP!

Shopman, Mr. Smith. Lorrident, Mr. Tye. Cobbler, Mr. Weft. Yokelsmith, Mrs. Robin. Bunchman, Mr. Winch. Chimney Mr. Wrighton ▓ Crabs & Paxolene
Breakfast, Illustration of Ply's celebrated Tale of Job. Death in Egypt, &c. Pylgrim. How to plate a Hare. Chase Fox, said to be in the
━━━ G━ R━ ━E ━ ━ ━T ━ ━ ━ ━ ━ ━T ━ ━

ACKNOWLEDGED BY MILLIONS!!!

Smith, Cheesemonger, 294, Oxford St. & Hairdressers
Barber, Mr. Park,.....One of the Indiscretions,—What a Whopping.

DUET BETWEEN THE CLOWN AND A ━━━
St. TURNOUR STREET

Drugstore, Messrs, Law and Order, Gearvasters, Messrs Tays and Fish, Policemen, Mr. Wrighton, Charpy Lawrence, Quick Setanes, and …

Nathan's Masquerade Warehouse, and Gun Makers!

LLOYD'S EMPORIUM OF KNOWLEDGE!

    Drastical Lecture, by a Spirit and the Plants— George Boy, Master Box

Road-side Public House & Blacksmith's Forge,
ON THE ROAD TO GRETNA.

Blacksmith, Mr. Hammersmaa. ——————— George Boy, Master Box

ELLIOTT London Porter, - - GRETNA-GREEN BLACKSMITH!
and the

COCKER'S GIGANTIC SLATES!

Harlequin goes through the Sums, and Clown assists a Question in Practice.
"You've worked the Sum, and now I will." "And thus the Wand, now the first is,
My promise of reward fulfil, By Cipher the owner, to practice,

THE REGIONS OF REWARDS.
W. R. BEVERLY

Scene Painters, - - - Messrs. W. R. BEVERLY & SCOTT, Leader W. CALCOTT.
Harlequin, Mr. MACKINTOSH, Stage Manager, - - Mr. BAKER.
Doors open at Half-past Six o'Clock.   The Performance commences at Seven. - - - - Second Price at Nine

☞ Children as Arms cannot be admitted.

The Box Office under the Superintendance of Mr. J. IVES, and will be open from 11 till 4 o'Clock.
IN ADDENDUM.]   G. Forward's, Printer T Exch House, Covent Garden.

Royal Olympic Theatre, c.1843.

Pork Chops

On Monday 13 February 1843 the 'Extravagant Entertainment' *Pork Chops; a Dream of Home* was presented for the first time at the Royal Olympic Theatre. The imminent arrival of the new play by Mr E.L. Blanchard was noted in typical punning fashion on the playbills for the previous week:

PORK CHOPS
Having had another *turn*, in order that they may be *well done*, will positively be served at Nine o'Clock NEXT MONDAY Night – The Public are invited to the Entertainment.'

Puns were very much the predilection of the play's author, Edward Leman Blanchard (1820-1889), who later specialised in writing pantomimes and 'Christmas Extravaganzas', producing at least one such entertainment a year from 1844 until his death. As drama critic of the Daily Telegraph for many years, Blanchard's *Pork Chops* was an early attempt at a form of drama

E.L. Blanchard and Madame Vestris.

of which he could later claim sovereignty, but as a 23 year-old playwright his creation was second item on the bill, 'Garnished with a DramATTIC Scene by Mr. W.R. Beverley And a Musical Sauce by Mr Calcott.' The rest of the evening contained sensational and melodramatic entertainment, as colourfully proclaimed in the playbill. Standards had certainly dropped at the Olympic since the former manager Madame Vestris had managed the theatre, from 1831 until 1839. Then she was praised by J.R. Planché because:

'You have never suffered your Play-bill to be disgraced by a puff, but rigidly restricted it to be a simple announcement of the performances.'

This playbill is certainly full of 'puff', or self-praise, and notes that 'half-price' was available at 9 o'clock. This refers to the popular 18th and 19th-century convention whereby those who came to the theatre for the second half of the evening were admitted at half price. The bill also notes proudly: 'By Authority of the Lord Chamberlain', since the management had been granted a licence to perform 'burletta' at the Olympic since 1813. Crammed with all this information, the playbill was unwieldy for the playgoers to handle, and it was large bills such as this that led to the introduction of theatre programmes later in the 19th-century.

Cheesy Cider Chops

8 pork chops
2 dessert apples or 1 large cooking apple
1 medium onion
2 oz (50 g) butter
½ pint (300 ml) dry cider
1 large tablespoon (1 × 15 ml spoon) plain flour
4 oz (100 g) mozzarella cheese
black pepper
salt

Peel and core the apples and slice quite finely. Peel and chop the onion. Melt the butter in a frying pan and gently fry the apple and onion for 5 minutes until soft but not brown. Sprinkle the flour into the pan, mix well, and add the cider. Cook for a further 5 minutes, adding salt and pepper. While this mixture is cooking, grill the chops on both sides until they are cooked and the fat is crisp. Transfer to a warmed serving dish and cover with the apple and onion mixture. Slice the mozzarella cheese finely and cover the top with the cheese. Return to the grill until the cheese is bubbling and golden. Serve at once, 2 chops for each serving.

Suggested wine: Valpolicella.

Gaiety Theatre.

Licensed by the Lord Chamberlain to Mr. GEORGE EDWARDES.

Manager ... ... Mr. GEORGE EDWARDES.

Mr. GEORGE EDWARDES

Will produce to-night (Tuesday, May 30th, 1905), at 8 o'clock, for the first time, a Musical Play,

The Spring - Chicken,

(Adapted from JAIME & DUVAL'S "Coquin de Printemps,")

BY

GEORGE GROSSMITH, JR.

Additional Lyrics by
ADRIAN ROSS
AND
PERCY GREENBANK.

Music by
IVAN CARYLL
AND
LIONEL MONCKTON.

Chorus line from *The Spring Chicken*. From 'The Sketch', 1906.

The Spring Chicken

With Gertie Millar as the beautiful leading lady and George Grossmith Jnr playing a flirtatious French lawyer, *The Spring Chicken* was presented by George Edwardes for the first time at the Gaiety Theatre on 30 May 1905.

An adaptation by Grossmith of the French play *Le Coquin de Printemps*, the main theme was marital infidelity, far more shocking in 1905 than today. With music by Ivan Caryll and Lionel Monckton and costumes by the prolific designer Wilhelm, *The Spring Chicken* proved to be another popular musical comedy for the Gaiety. Grossmith's character, Babori, was created as a satirical protrayal of the lawyer in the Dreyfus Affair, Maitre Labori, but the political references were less important than the risqué ones and than the tuneful score, which ensured full houses at the Gaiety for 401 performances.

At the old Gaiety Theatre, closed for demolition in July 1903 to facilitate the widening of the Strand, and the new Gaiety, which opened four months later, George Edwardes established and refined the successful formula of musical comedy. Providing beautiful girls, tuneful music and witty comedy, Edwardes followed in the footsteps of his previous employer D'Oyly Carte at the Savoy and attracted society audiences to his theatres. The 'Gaiety Girls' became famous for their looks – reproduced in numerous postcards – and several of them married into the peerage. Known as 'The Guv'nor', Edwardes was a popular and successful entrepreneur, keeping stars like Gertie Millar, Edmund Payne, Connie Ediss and Grossmith Jnr with his Company for many years.

George Grossmith Jun. as Gustave Babori.
From 'The Sketch', 1905.

Chicken with Grape Sauce

1 chicken (3-4 lbs; 1.4-1.8 kg)

SAUCE
8 oz (225 g) white grapes
1 pint (600 ml) chicken stock
2 oz (50 g) butter
2 oz (50 g) plain flour
2 egg yolks
1 wineglass white wine
black pepper
salt

STUFFING
1 medium onion
2 oz (50 g) mushrooms
2 oz (50 g) fresh white breadcrumbs
1 oz (25 g) butter
1 orange
1 lemon
½ teaspoon (½ × 5 ml spoon) thyme
black pepper
salt

Wipe and pat the chicken dry. To make the stuffing, peel and chop the onion, and wipe and chop the mushrooms. Melt 1 oz (25 g) butter in a frying pan. Fry the onions gently for 3 minutes until soft and add the mushrooms for a further 2 minutes. Sprinkle on the thyme, salt and pepper. Grate the rinds of the orange and lemon and reserve for the sauce. Squeeze the juice of half the lemon and put in a bowl with the chopped flesh of the orange and remaining half lemon. Add the breadcrumbs and the onion and mushroom mixture. Combine these ingredients throughly and stuff the bird. Dot the chicken with butter and cook in a roasting tin in a hot oven (400°F, 200°C, gas mark 6) for 15 minutes to the lb (450 g) plus 15 minutes. Baste regularly.

To make the sauce, melt 2 oz (50 g) butter in a saucepan, mixing 2 oz (50 g) plain flour into the butter and cooking gently for 1 minute. Add the chicken stock (which can be made from a stock cube) and the white wine gradually, mixing well and cooking until the sauce is smooth and thick. Halve the grapes and remove the pips. Add them to the sauce with some of the meat juices from the roasting tin. Season to taste and beat in two egg yolks, and the reserved orange and lemon rinds, grated.

Carve the bird; put some stuffing with each serving and pour over a generous amount of the sauce before serving.

Suggested wine: A young red Beaujolais, such as Fleurie.

The Pigeon

Wilfred Shine, Margaret Morris and Whitford Kane in *The Pigeon*. From 'The Sporting and Dramatic News', 1912.

Preceded by a 'curtain-raiser' – as *In the Soup* had been twelve years previously – *The Pigeon* opened at the Royalty Theatre on 30 January 1912. 'A Fantasy in Three Acts' by John Galsworthy, the play concerned a philanthropic artist who fed and clothed some 'down and outs', sharing his home with them. Whitford Kane played the artist Christopher Wellwyn, seen as 'the pigeon', sheltering wild birds. His daughter Ann, who reprimanded him for his generosity, was played by the ravishing Gladys Cooper.

In the curtain-raiser *The Constant Lover*, Denis Eadie, actor-manager at the Royalty Theatre, played opposite Gladys

Cooper. In *The Pigeon* he appeared as Ferrand. It was he and his co-manager, J.E. Vedrenne, who had given Gladys Cooper a three-year contract to appear at the Royalty after an earlier engagement there in 1911. Miss Cooper's previous London appearances had been in musical comedy, especially at the Gaiety Theatre from 1907, singing in the chorus when the stars were Gertie Millar and George Grossmith. The parts which Gladys Cooper played at the Royalty established her reputation as a straight actress instead of just a singing 'postcard beauty'. Acclaimed for her role in *Milestones* at the Royalty in March 1912, Gladys Cooper later remembered: 'I worked harder at the Royalty than I have ever worked in my life.'

John Galsworthy wrote his first play *The Silver Box* in 1906, by which time he was already known as a socially conscious novelist. *The Pigeon* followed *Strife*, 1909, and *Justice*, 1910, which contributed to his reputation as one of the country's most important contemporary dramatists, along with Shaw and Granville-Barker.

Pigeons in Cider

4 pigeons
1 large onion
8 oz (225 g) streaky bacon
8 oz (225 g) mushrooms
1 bayleaf
1 pint (600 ml) dry cider
3 oz (75 g) butter
1 tablespoon (1 × 15 ml spoon) plain flour
salt
black pepper

Peel and chop the onion. Wipe and chop the mushrooms. Cut off the bacon rinds which can be grilled until crisp and served as a savoury nibble with drinks before dinner. Chop the bacon. Melt 2 oz (50 g) butter in a frying pan. Fry the onion and bacon for 5 minutes until soft. Add the mushrooms and fry gently for another 3 minutes. Season. Remove from the pan and reserve.

Melt another ounce (25 g) butter in the frying pan and brown the pigeons all over. Place them in an ovenproof casserole dish. Add the vegetables and bacon, pour over the cider, add the bayleaf and cook, covered, in a moderate oven (350°F, 180°C, gas mark 4) for 2 hours. When the pigeons are ready, place on a serving dish with the vegetables, removing and discarding the bayleaf. Keep the pigeons warm. In a cup, blend the tablespoon (15 ml spoon) plain flour with the tablespoon of juices from the casserole dish. Put the rest of the juices in a saucepan, add the flour mixture and heat gently, stirring all the time, until the sauce has thickened. Adjust the seasoning and pour over the pigeons. Serve immediately.

Suggested wine: St Emilion or Pomerol.

Aldwych Theatre
STRAND

| 24 Pages | THE MAGAZINE PROGRAMME | 24 Pages |

TOM WALLS and RALPH LYNN

TOM WALLS and REGINALD HIGHLEY, Ltd.

present

"TURKEY TIME"

A New Farce in Three Acts

By BEN TRAVERS

Turkey Time

Ben Travers knew how to keep an audience laughing. As he once said:

'The whole secret of farce is that it's about ordinary people in ordinary situations: if it happens to a bunch of clowns, it isn't funny at all.'

Travers' first play, The Dippers, was produced at the Criterion Theatre in 1922 but his next play A Cuckoo in the Nest, found a very friendly home in the Aldwych Theatre, from July 1925. Travers was to become the most prosperous dramatist of his day, making his name from the series of farces which ran at the Aldwych from 1925 until 1933 and which became universally known as 'the Aldwych Farces.'

Turkey Time, the seventh Travers farce to be presented at the Aldwych, opened on 26 May 1931 and achieved a run of 263 performances. Its cast consisted of what was virtually to become the stock company – Tom Walls, Ralph Lynn, Robertson Hare, Alfred Drayton, Winifred Shotter, Mary Brough and Yvonne Arnaud. Thereafter Travers wrote with these actors in mind, always ensuring that they would find themselves in picaresque situations and that whichever unfortunate character was played by Robertson Hare would find himself a victim of something or other – his famous catchphrase being 'Oh, calamity!' Ralph Lynn specialised in the 'silly ass' roles, complete with monocle and protruding teeth. Travers once dubbed Lynn, a great favourite of the public, 'the greatest farce actor of the century.'

Travers always claimed that he learned the secrets of farcical timing from studying the work of the playwright Pinero, and he prided himself on the fact that:

'I have never written in my plays a single entrance or exit of any character at any time when they didn't come from somewhere with a reasonable purpose or go somewhere because they have got to go. In Feydeau they all come bouncing out of bedrooms in all directions.'

Travers died in December 1980 at the age of 94, his last play The Bed Before Yesterday having received its première in 1975. Asked the following year if he was considering writing any more plays, Travers replied:

'Maybe. . . . but I think I'd like that one to be produced posthumously so if it's a success I can smile down benignly from the clouds and if it's a failure I shan't have to read the notices.'

Norma Varden and J. Robertson Hare (left); Ralph Lynn and Winifred Shotter (right), in *Turkey Time*. Opposite, the members of the cast.

Turkey Fillets in Sherry

4 turkey fillets
1 large 14 oz (400 g) tin tomatoes
20 stuffed olives
2 tablespoons (2 × 15 ml) dry sherry
2 cloves garlic
1 medium onion
4 oz (100 g) mushrooms
2 oz (50 g) butter
1 oz (25 g) plain flour
¼ pint (150 ml) double cream
black pepper
salt

Place the turkey fillets in a bowl. Slice the stuffed olives. Remove the papery coating from the cloves of garlic and chop finely with a little salt. Add olives and garlic to the bowl with the tin of tomatoes and their juice, sherry and salt and pepper. Leave the meat to marinate in this mixture for at least an hour. Melt the butter in a frying pan. Remove the turkey fillets from the marinade and cook them quickly on both sides to seal the meat. Place the meat in an ovenproof casserole dish. Peel and chop the onions. Wipe and chop the mushrooms. Fry the onions gently in the butter for 3 minutes until soft and add the mushrooms for a futher 2 minutes. Put the onion and mushrooms in the casserole with the meat. Add the marinade mixture and cook in a medium oven (350°F, 180°C, gas mark 4) for 20 minutes. Place the meat on a serving dish and keep warm. In a cup, blend the flour with a tablespoon of the juice from the casserole. Pour the rest of the casserole juice into a saucepan. Add the flour mixture. Heat the sauce gently, stirring constantly until thickened. Stir in the cream. Test the seasoning and pour the mixture over the turkey fillets. Serve immediately.

Suggested wine: A red Rioja.

Noel Coward and Gertrude Lawrence as George and Lily Pepper. Cartoon by Tom Titt from 'The Tatler', 1936.

Noel Coward, c. 1935.

Red Peppers

'In the year 1935, upheld by my stubborn faith in the "star system" I wrote the *To-Night at 8.30* plays as acting, singing and dancing vehicles for Gertrude Lawrence and myself. The success we had had with *Private Lives* both in London and New York encouraged me to believe that the public liked to see us playing together, and this belief, happily for both of us and the managements concerned, turned out to be fully justified.'

Noel Coward, the boy actor in *The Goldfish*, 1911, first made his name as a playwright with a serious work, *The Vortex*, 1924. His versatility was demonstrated by such plays as *Hay Fever*, (1925) *Private Lives*, (1930) and musicals including *This Year of Grace*, (1928) and *Bitter-Sweet*, (1929). By writing and producing *Tonight at 8.30*, Coward wanted to reinstate the short play to the popularity it had enjoyed in the 19th-century, his primary object: 'to provide a full and varied evening's entertainment.'

First presented in a programme called *To-Night at 7.30* at the Manchester Opera House on 15 October 1935, *Red Peppers* was accompanied by two other short plays called *We Were Dancing* and *The Astonished Heart*. Opening in London at the Phoenix Theatre on 9 January 1936, *Family Album* and *The Astonished Heart* joined *Red Peppers*. Another triple bill, presented the following evening, completed the work.

In *Red Peppers*, Gertrude Lawrence and Noel Coward played the vaudeville performers George and Lily Pepper whose lives involved provincial tours and back-stage bickering. The curtain rises on George and Lily performing their tacky number 'Has Anybody See our Ship?', and after a heated argument in an intervening 'off-stage' scene, the couple return to perform their last number, 'Man About Town', during which their aggrieved musical director increases the tempo mercilessly.

The Phoenix Theatre had witnessed the triumph of Noel and Gertie in *Private Lives* and five years later it again brought them luck for *To-Night at 8.30*. As one critic noted the day after the première:

'It was a Noel Coward festival at the Phoenix Theatre last night – a success of brilliance both on stage and off, and enthusiasm everywhere!'

Stuffed Peppers

4 red peppers
1 medium onion
4 oz (100 g) mushrooms
7 oz (175 g) chicken livers
1 tablespoon (1 × 15 ml spoon) tomato purée
¼ pint (150 ml) soured cream
2 oz (50 g) butter
½ teaspoon (½ × 5 ml spoon) mixed herbs
black pepper
salt

Peel and chop the onion. Wipe and chop the mushrooms. Melt the butter in a frying pan. Fry the onions gently in the butter for 3 minutes until soft. Add the mushrooms and the chicken livers, and cook for a further 3 minutes. Season with salt and pepper and add the mixed herbs, tomato purée and soured cream.

Wash the peppers, cut the tops off each, and carefully remove the seeds. Cut a sliver from the bottom of each pepper so that they stand upright. Stand the peppers in a baking tin, with a little hot water in the bottom of the tin. Pile the filling mixture into the peppers and cook in a moderate oven (350°F, 180°C, gas mark 4) for 1½ hours.

Suggested wine: Côtes du Rhône.

PRINCES THEATRE
Shaftesbury Avenue, W.C.2
Licensed by the Lord Chamberlain to - - BERT E. HAMMOND

FIRTH SHEPHARD

presents

"SHEPHARD'S PIE"

Cartoons by Tom Titt from 'The Tatler', 1940.

Richard Hearne as the Scoutmaster with (left to right) Jack Leopold, Sydney Howard and Arthur Riscoe as evacuees in the sketch 'Evacuees'.

Shephard's Pie

With food rationing already in force over Christmas 1939, the British public wanted good meals as well as good entertainment to cheer themselves out of the growing wartime gloom. At the Prince's Theatre the manager Firth Shephard provided the entertainment with the very funny revue by Douglas Furber, to which Shephard lent his name. It opened on 21 December 1939 and achieved a run of 356 performances.

Shephard's Pie was well reviewed. Critics praised the sketches and songs, noting that the audience particularly liked the sketch in which Arthur Riscoe performed a burlesque as Hitler, and was blown to pieces! Two of the actors singled out for praise were Phyllis Robins who 'was almost wearing a white dress', and the 'inspired' Richard Hearne, who became known to a later generation as television's 'Mr Pastry'.

The Prince's Theatre, which opened in December 1911 as the New Prince's was situated on the corner of High Holborn and Shaftesbury Avenue. Closed for renovation in 1936 it reopened in March 1963 as the Shaftesbury Theatre, the name it bears today. Successes at the Shaftesbury have included Sarah Bernhardt in *Daniel* (1921) and the rock musical *Hair* (1968) but comedy always seems to have had a special place in the history of the theatre, which today is the home for the excellent Theatre of Comedy Company.

Shephard's Pie was described in 1939 as 'a lively and well-staged show', and Philip Page wrote of it: 'Here is a most delectable pie.'

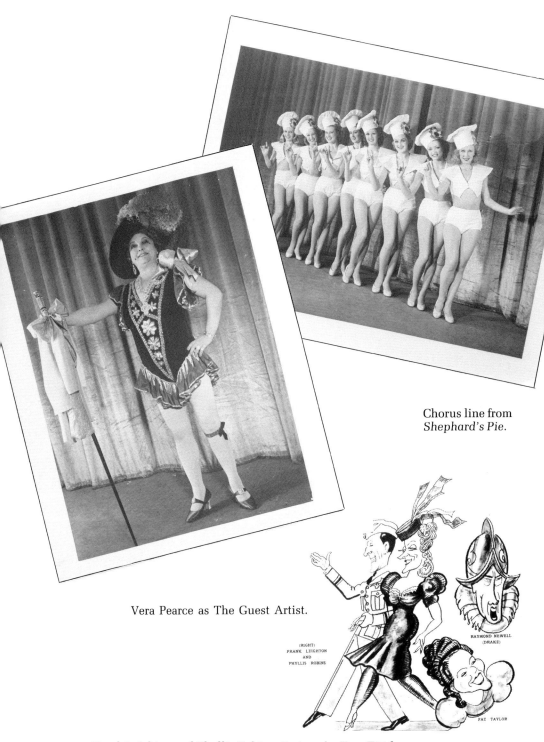

Chorus line from *Shephard's Pie*.

Vera Pearce as The Guest Artist.

Frank Leighton and Phyllis Robins. Cartoon by Tom Titt from 'The Tatler', 1940.

Vera Pearce in *Shephard's Pie*. Cartoon by Tom Titt from 'The Tatler', 1940.

Shepherd's Pie

1 lb (450 g) mince
1 large onion
1 medium green pepper
4 oz (100 g) mushrooms
4 oz (100 g) carrots
4 oz (100 g) peas
small tin tomato purée
1 clove garlic
2 oz (50 g) butter
dash Worcester sauce

black pepper
salt

TOPPING
2 lbs (1 kg) potatoes
2 oz (50 g) butter
¼ pint (150 ml) milk
½ teaspoon (½ × 5 ml spoon) mustard powder
salt
black pepper

Peel and slice the onion. Remove papery coating from the clove of garlic and chop finely with a little salt. Remove the seeds from the green pepper. Wash and chop the flesh. Wipe and chop the mushrooms. Melt 2 oz (50 g) butter in a frying pan and fry the onion and green pepper for 3 minutes until soft. Add the mushrooms, mince, pepper and salt, and continue cooking for a further 5 minutes. Peel and chop the carrots and cook in boiling salted water for 10 minutes, adding the peas for the last 3 minutes. Drain the vegetables and add to the meat and onion mixture, with tomato purée and a dash of Worcester sauce.

Peel and chop the potatoes. Cook in boiling water for 20 minutes until soft. Drain and mash with the milk, butter and mustard powder, salt and pepper. When the topping is smooth and creamy, transfer the meat mixture into an ovenproof casserole dish. Top with the creamed potatoes and cook in a medium oven (375°F, 190°C, gas mark 5) for 30 minutes.

Suggested wine: A red Chateauneuf-du-Pape.

'The Distracted Family' in *Little Lambs Eat Ivy*. Cartoon by Tom Titt from 'The Tatler', 1948.

Little Lambs Eat Ivy

'All the signs are that Noel Langley's new play "Little Lambs Eat Ivy" at the Ambassadors, is a smash hit. It is a wild affair, exaggerated to the pitch of peril; but it comes off, and in the theatre that is all that matters. If it had been less cleverly written, less deftly produced, less carefully cast, and less brilliantly acted, I might have been writing a very acid notice now.'

So W.A. Darlington began his review of *Little Lambs Eat Ivy*, which opened at the Ambassadors Theatre on 8 April 1948. The critics agreed that it was not a marvellous play but that it was very well done, with 'fun as light as a feather' and 'happy touches' that made it wonderfully good entertainment.

Set in Lady Buckering's house near Regent's Park, the play revolved around her 'near certifiable' family, and showed their affairs and concerns during one very argumentative Saturday. Lady Buckering, a widow, played by Joan Hawthorne, owes her landlord a substantial amount of rent. Three of her daughters are periodically hysterical, while the fourth is having a baby upstairs. Husbands and wives quarrel in front of the dispassionate butler, while the nurse and doctor occupy themselves with the expectant mother despite the surrounding chaos.

Little Lambs Eat Ivy undoubtedly provided an amusing evening's entertainment, but with its title taken from the popular wartime nonsense song, it was the sort of commercial insubstantial theatrical fare that young writers like Osborne and Pinter reacted against a few years later. In 1948, however, audiences thoroughly enjoyed Noel Langley's play into which he had dropped jokes: 'with the free hand of a good-natured cook making a pre-war plum cake for the nursery'. It ran successfully at the Ambassadors Theatre for 379 performances.

Lamb Chops en Croûte

4 lamb chump chops
1 large onion
8 oz (225 g) mushrooms
2 tablespoons (2 × 15 ml spoons) French or German mustard
1 tablespoon (1 × 15 ml spoon) parsley
1 tablespoon (1 × 15 ml spoon) tarragon
2 oz (50 g) butter
black pepper
salt

SHORTCRUST PASTRY
1 lb (450 g) plain flour
8 oz (225 g) butter
1 teaspoon (1 × 5 ml spoon) salt
2 tablespoons (2 × 15 ml spoons) water
1 tablespoon (1 × 15 ml spoon) lemon juice
beaten egg for glaze

Cut out the little bone from the chops and trim off any surplus fat. Heat the butter in a frying pan and brown the chops quickly on both sides, just to seal the meat. Remove from the pan and leave to cool. Peel and chop the onion finely. Wipe and chop the mushrooms. Fry the onion gently in the butter until soft for 3 minutes, adding the mushrooms for a further 2 minutes. Season this mixture with salt and pepper and leave to cool. Chop the parsley and tarragon and mix with the mustard.

While the meat and filling are cooling, make the shortcrust pastry by sieving the flour with the salt into a bowl. Add the butter, cut into small pieces, and rub it into the flour with the fingertips until the mixture resembles breadcrumbs. Pour the water and lemon juice into a well in the centre of the mixture and blend with a fork into a dough. Place on a lightly floured surface and knead gently. Leave in a cool place to rest for 15 minutes before rolling with a lightly floured rolling pin. Place a chop on the pastry and cut round the shape of the meat to make a base for a chop. Spread the chop with mustard mixture and a quarter of the onion and mushroom mixture. Cut a larger piece for the cover of the pastry case and seal the pastry round the edges. Repeat the process for each chop. Decorate the pastry cases with any remaining pastry. Glaze with the beaten egg and cook in a hot oven (400°F, 200°C, gas mark 6) on a baking tray for 25 minutes, until the pastry is golden.

Suggested wine: Château Mouton-Rothschild or, (rather cheaper), Mouton-Cadet.

SAVILLE THEATRE
SHAFTESBURY AVENUE, W.C.2. TEMPLE BAR 4011
Proprietors: S.T.P. (Theatres) Ltd.

Licensed by the Lord Chamberlain to John Clements

JOHN CLEMENTS
presents
FOR EIGHT WEEKS ONLY
21st DECEMBER, 1955 to 18th FEBRUARY, 1956

EMLYN WILLIAMS

DOROTHY TUTIN

ANGELA BADDELEY

GEORGE RELPH

MICHAEL GOUGH

THE WILD DUCK

By HENRIK IBSEN   Adapted by MAX FABER

CHARLES CARSON
PEGGY LIVESEY

ROBERT BEAUMONT
GRAHAM STUART

LAURENCE HARDY

Directed by MURRAY MACDONALD
Settings and Costumes by LAURENCE IRVING

EVENINGS AT 7.30
WEDNESDAYS AND SATURDAYS AT 2.30

The Wild Duck

When Ibsen's plays were first produced in England, between 1891 and 1897, critics detested them. One reviewer described Ibsen as:

'A dramatist who, apart from the non-construction of his alleged plays, deliberately selects his subjects from the most sordid, abject, even the most revolting corners of human life.'

Victorian audiences were not, on the whole, attuned to realistic plays dealing frankly with contemporary problems, and although Ibsen's work was defended by Edmund Gosse and his translator William Archer, this hostile reaction was typical.

The Norwegian dramatist wrote *The Wild Duck* in 1884 and it was first produced in Norway in January 1885. The first English production, at the Royalty Theatre on 5 May 1894, with Winifred Fraser as Hedvig, was by J.T. Grien's Independent Theatre – the group that first brought Shaw's plays to the attention of the public. As a private theatre club organised on a subscription basis, the Independent could produce plays not licensed by the Lord Chamberlain. Their production of Ibsen's *Ghosts* three years before had aroused a fierce critical storm.

Gradually Ibsen's plays became recognised as subtle and brilliant works, and when *The Wild Duck* was produced at the St Martin's Theatre on 3 November 1948, Anthony Cookman wrote:

'We are there shown that *The Wild Duck* is as exquisitely comic as it is exquisitely pathetic.'

Fay Compton played Gina Ekdal in that production, with Robert Harris as Gregers Werle and Mai Zetterling as Hedvig. Michael Benthall directed the production which received unanimous critical acclaim. A later notable production at the Saville Theatre in December 1956 starred Emlyn Williams as Hjalmar with Angela Baddeley as Gina and Dorothy Tutin as Hedvig. Miss Tutin's portrayal of heart-breaking trust and candour was declared by one critic to be 'amazing to watch.'

In the 1979 National Theatre production, using a version of the text translated by Christopher Hampton, Ekdal was played by Ralph Richardson with Yvonne Bryceland and Eva Griffith as Gina and Hedvig.

Dorothy Tutin as Hedvig. Saville Theatre, 1956.

Mallard with Cointreau and Cream Sauce

2 good-sized mallard
3 oranges
1 lemon
¼ pint (150 ml) stock
1 tablespoon (1 × 15 ml spoon) clear honey
2 tablespoons (2 × 15 ml spoons) Cointreau
1 tablespoon (1 × 15 ml spoon) plain flour
1 medium onion
black pepper
salt
¼ pint (150 ml) single cream
bunch of watercress

If the butcher has given you the giblets, make some stock by covering them with cold water in a saucepan, adding a bouquet garni, bringing to the boil and simmering for 20 minutes. Strain, and reserve for sauce. If no giblets, make ¼ pint (150 ml) stock with a chicken stock cube.

Wash the duck. Pat it dry, and stuff with one of the oranges (peeled) and the onion, peeled. Put the duck in a roasting tin. Season and add the stock to the roasting tin. Cook in a medium oven (375°F, 190°C gas mark 5). After the first 10 minutes, baste the bird and add the honey to the juices in the pan. Baste again. Cook for a further 40 minutes, basting regularly.

Grate the rinds from 1 orange and the lemon, and squeeze their juices. Slice the remaining orange for garnish, and wash the watercress. When the duck is cooked with the skin nicely crisp, put it on a serving dish and keep warm. Pour off the excess fat from the roasting tin and mix the tablespoon of flour with the fruit juices until smooth. Add this to the pan with the grated rinds and tablespoons of Cointreau. Simmer, stirring constantly, until thickened. Add the cream and heat gently. Season to taste. Arrange orange slices and watercress round the bird and serve the sauce separately, putting some of the garnish on each plate when the bird is carved.

Suggested wine: A red Burgundy such as Nuits St Georges or (cheaper), red Macon.

DANCING ON THE CEILING

CHARLES·B·COCHRAN'S PRODUCTION

EVER GREEN

A MUSICAL PLAY BY
BENN LEVY

Lyrics by
LORENZ HART
Music by
RICHARD RODGERS

VOCAL NUMBERS	net.
In the Cool of the Evening	2/-
Dancing on the Ceiling	2/-
Dear! Dear!	2/-
If I give in to you	2/-
No place but Home	2/-
Pianoforte Selection	2/6

CHAPPELL & Cº LTD
50, NEW BOND ST LONDON, W.I.
NEW YORK & SYDNEY
PRINTED IN ENGLAND

Ever Green

On the evening of 3 December 1930 the curtain rose at the newly reconstructed Adelphi Theatre for Mr Charles B. Cochran's latest spectacular production, Ever Green. Described as a 'musical show', it was based on the book by Benn Levy with lyrics by Lorenz Hart and music by Richard Rodgers. The three-hour performance starred Jessie Matthews, Jean Cadell, Sonnie Hale, and Kay Hammond. It also featured the acrobats Carlos and Chita, the dancer Joyce Barbour, the John Tiller Girls, and Mr Cochran's Young Ladies. Ten designers worked on the costumes and sets, including Ernst Stern, Gladys Calthrop, Doris Zinkeisen and Rex Whistler, and the stage revolved to present twelve different sets ranging from a French circus scene to a Spanish village. As Ivor Brown wrote in his review:

'Mr Cochran's insatiable appetite for showmanship which is exquisite as well as expensive has run gloriously mad . . . Mr Cochran has decided to go the whole Hollywood. . .'

The Hollywood connection was also noted by the reviewer of The News Chronicle who decided:

'. . . theatrical history was made last night in the new and beautifully decorated Adelphi Theatre. With his genius as a showman, C.B. Cochran has struck a shrewd blow against its rival, the cinema.'

Called Ever Green because the beautiful Harriet Green, played by Jessie Matthews, was supposed to be an eternally youthful 60 year-old, the production was more a revue with a plot than a narrative musical show. Indeed Cochran was the acknowledged master of revue, having presented one annually at the London Pavilion from 1918 until 1931. His flair for the spectacular had been evident in his first great theatrical success, The Miracle, which he had presented at Olympia in 1911, with Max Reinhardt. 'Cocky', as he was nicknamed, always wanted the best, and he knew how to achieve it. He could recognise and nurture talent, as he did when he was impressed by the 23 year-old Noel Coward, and his association with Coward led to successes including Bitter Sweet (1929) and Private Lives (1930). He also introduced to the British stage the musical talents of Richard Rodgers, Cole Porter and Jerome Kern. He received a knighthood for his services to the theatre in 1948, three years before his death at the age of seventy-nine.

Jessie Matthews as Harriet Green, and the chorus line from *Ever Green*.

Spinach Roulade with Onion Cream Filling

FOR THE SPINACH ROLL
2 oz (50 g) butter
2 oz (50 g) plain flour
¼ pint (150 ml) milk
1 teaspoon mustard powder
salt, black pepper
4 egg yolks
3 egg whites
1 lb (450 g) defrosted frozen spinach

FOR THE FILLING
1 oz (25 g) butter
1 medium onion, finely chopped
2 tablespoons soured cream
½ teaspoon dill weed
salt
black pepper

To make the spinach roll, melt 2 oz (50 g) butter over a low heat in a saucepan. Add the flour and cook gently for one minute, stirring constantly. Remove from the heat, add the milk and cook over a low heat, beating all the time until you have a smooth, thick sauce. Add the teaspoon of mustard powder, a little salt and black pepper. Remove from the heat and leave to cool.

While this is cooling, butter a swiss roll tin and line it with greaseproof paper, leaving about 2 in (5 cm) extra paper overlapping each edge of the tin. Butter the paper, smoothing the greaseproof into the edges of the tin so that it fits snugly. Separate the eggs. Add four egg yolks to the white sauce, beating well, and then add the unfrozen spinach. Mix well. Beat the three egg whites and fold in the spinach mixture, combining the two thoroughly.

Pour the mixture into the swiss roll tin and cook in a medium oven (350°F, 180°C, gas mark 4), for fifteen minutes.

To make the filling, melt 1 oz (25 g) butter gently over a low heat in a frying pan. Add the chopped onion and fry gently till softened. Add the dill, salt and black pepper. Remove from the heat and add two tablespoons of soured cream.

When the roulade is cooked, take it out of the oven and allow it to cool for a few minutes. Spread the onion mixture evenly over the top. Gently roll up the roulade as you would a swiss roll, using the overlapping greaseproof paper at one end of the tin to help lift it. Serve cut into slices.

If you wish to make this in advance, wrap the finished roulade in greased silver foil. Reheat for about twenty minutes in a moderate oven (350°F, 180°C, gas mark 4).

This is delicious served as a vegetable with a plain meat or fish dish. It can also be served hot or cold as a starter; you can vary the fillings. It is also delicious spread with a cream cheese or taramasalata filling, or strips of each.

Edith Evans, Cedric Hardwicke and Louis Hampton in *The Late Christopher Bean*. Cover from 'The Play Pictorial', 1933.

The Late Christopher Bean

Adapted by Emlyn Williams from a comedy by René Fauchois originally entitled 'Prenez Garde à la Peinture,' *The Late Christopher Bean* opened at the St James's Theatre on 16 May 1933. The plot revolves around a doctor who has been left a bundle of paintings by an old friend, the impecunious and somewhat alcoholic artist Christopher Bean. When art critics and dealers arrive at the doctor's door clamouring to buy the works, the doctor realises their value and tries to discover where he abandoned them. Was it in the attic? Or even the chicken run? He wants to sell them all – even that given by Bean to his Welsh maid, Gwenny. She refuses, leaves the doctor's service and reveals that she is not just the only one who truly values the paintings, but is also Christopher's widow.

The casting of the play was excellent, with Cedric Hardwicke as the doctor, Louise Hampton as his harrassed wife, and Edith Evans as Gwenny, playing sensitively 'with a beauty and quiet drive that would glorify tragedy.' The dialogue was praised as 'sparkling', and as one critic wrote:

'From the moment the curtain rang up at the St James last night on *The Late Christopher Bean* the audience chuckled so frequently that hardly anyone could hear all the jokes.'

Critics were unanimous in praise of the production. A comedy with a touch of fantasy, it ran for over a year, and introduces a recipe suitably using runner beans!

Robert Holmes as Tallant and Edith Evans as Gwenny.

Cartoon by Haselden of Cedric Hardwicke
in *The Late Christopher Bean*, 1933.

French Beans with Tomatoes

1 lb (450 g) young runner beans, topped and tailed but left whole
1 clove garlic
1 medium onion
1 small tin tomatoes
1 oz (25 g) butter
1 oz (25 g) walnuts
black pepper
salt
sprig of parsley

Melt the butter in a frying pan. Remove the papery coating from the clove of garlic and chop finely, with a little salt. Peel and chop the onion. Cook the garlic and onion with the chopped parsley in the butter for 5 minutes, until soft. Chop the walnuts and add to the pan. Empty the tin of tomatoes in the pan. Add the beans. Simmer for 10 minutes and serve.

The Magic Cabbage

Cabbages are really roses belonging to the last green giantess on earth – or so the programme for *The Magic Cabbage* told children who came to see it at the Unicorn Theatre Club at the Arts Theatre. With music by Nic Rowley, Stephen Wyatt's fantasy opened there on 25 February 1978. The play concerned a girl called Jenny who couldn't cook or eat the magic cabbage, but who spent her birthday chasing the elusive vegetable, meeting a magician and various talking animals along the way. This was one of the imaginative and lively productions staged at weekends specially for children by the Unicorn Theatre.

A professional group, Unicorn was founded by Caryl Jenner as a touring company in 1948, and moved to its present home, the Arts Theatre, in 1968. Currently under the artistic direction of Chris Wallis, the Unicorn also organises workshops for children from the age of four, on topics including musical stories, puppets, tumbling, magic, make-up and stage-fighting. They produce a regular newsletter with competitions as well as information on workshops and productions.

Unicorn is one of the few groups of professional actors in London working exclusively for children. They understand the necessary techniques involved in entertaining young audiences, and know how demanding and discriminating they can be. Children are much less inhibited than adults and become totally involved in a production, participating as much as they did in Ken Whitmore's *Jump*, presented at the Unicorn in 1976. In the finale, the whole audience were asked to jump to save the world – and invariably, did.

Cabbage with Bacon

This makes an ideal accompaniment to plain roast or grilled meat.

½ large, or 1 small head of cabbage
4 rashers of streaky bacon
2 medium onions
1 oz (25 g) butter
½ wineglass sherry
pinch of nutmeg
black pepper
salt

Chop the bacon and fry it gently in its own fat, adding a little butter if it sticks to the pan. When slightly crisp, add the remaining butter and the finely shredded or chopped onion, and cook gently until the onion is soft. Add the finely chopped cabbage and stir-fry until it is sufficiently soft. (This entirely depends on how crunchy you like your cabbage.) Season with salt and pepper and a pinch of nutmeg. Finally, raise the heat a little and pour the sherry over the mixture. Stir well, and serve hot.

Sept. 23, 1938.

SHAFTESBURY THEATRE

Leslie Banks as Mr Chips with John Hepworth as Colley.

"GOODBYE, MR. CHIPS"

Constance Cummings as Katherine and Leslie Banks as Mr Chips.

PROGRAMME

Goodbye, Mr Chips

'An honest and quiet play', *Goodbye, Mr Chips* was originally presented at the old Shaftesbury Theatre on 22 September 1938. The story of Mr Chipping's career, written by James Hilton, had first appeared in 1934 as a serial in a magazine. After it was published in novel form James Hilton and Barbara Burnham adapted it for the stage.

Leslie Banks played the schoolmaster Mr Chips whose career at Brookfield School is traced from the time that he first takes 'prep' as a nervous young master of twenty-two, to his life as an experienced teacher of forty, newly married to a beautiful wife, played by Constance Cummings. She dies tragically in childbirth, and years later we see Mr Chips, now retired, in shabby academic gown returning to the school to teach in the First World War, after the young masters have enlisted. One scene shows him stoically taking a Latin lesson despite a German bombing raid, while in another he is seen as the much-loved master serving tea and walnut cake to his pupils. Leslie Banks had the task of ageing almost sixty years during the play. As one critic decided:

'Mr Chips had a beautiful nature, but not as beautiful as Mr. Banks' interpretation of it.'

Among the forty performers in the production, Constance Cummings' portrayal of the young wife was particularly noted. The success of the stage play led to a film version the following year, by which time James Hilton had emigrated to California, where he died in 1954.

Potatoes au Gratin

1 lb (450 g) potatoes
1 medium onion
4 oz (100 g) Gruyère cheese
½ pint (150 ml) milk
1 oz (25 g) butter
¼ teaspoon (¼ × 5 ml spoon)
dry mustard
black pepper
salt

Peel the potatoes and slice them thinly. Place them in a bowl. Cover with cold water and allow to soak for a few minutes. Peel and chop the onion and grate the cheese. Drain the potatoes and lightly grease a fireproof dish with a little of the butter. Layer the potatoes, cheese and onion in the dish, finishing with a layer of cheese. Mix the mustard, pepper and salt with the milk and pour over the dish. Dot the topping with the remaining butter and cook in a fairly hot oven (375°F, 190°C, gas mark 5) for an hour.

Joan Plowright as Beatie Bryant with Gwen Nelson as her mother, Royal Court Theatre, 1959.

Roots

'There was a point when I actually gave up writing. I was getting rejection slips. I got depressed. I was twenty-one. "You're not a writer", I told myself. "You never will be. You're finished. All right, you're a kitchen porter, you can learn a trade, you can be happy." But somehow you can't run away from yourself like that. I became involved with the people in the kitchen, the conflict came up again, and I'd make notes, cheating myself into thinking I wasn't really writing. Then I wrote *Chicken Soup with Barley* and I suddenly knew that this was it. I knew it all the time. And that's how I became a playwright.'

– Arnold Wesker.

Chicken Soup with Barley (1958) was the first work in the Wesker trilogy which also comprised *Roots* (1959) and *I'm*

Talking About Jerusalem (1960). The production of these plays in London owed much to George Devine who had founded the English Stage Company at the Royal Court Theatre in 1956, to promote new English works and foreign plays not previously produced in London. After John Osborne's *Look Back in Anger* was produced there on 8 May 1956, Wesker said:

'When I saw it, I just recognised that things *could* be done in the theatre and immediately went home and wrote *Chicken Soup*.'

After *Chicken Soup* was produced at the Royal Court Theatre in July 1958, Wesker was comissioned to finish his next play, *Roots*. Despite Devine's doubts about the structure of the play, Joan Plowright's desire to perform in it induced the Belgrade Theatre, Coventry to mount it. It was subsequently produced at the Royal Court Theatre on 30 June 1959.

The trilogy deals with the life of the Khan family, Sarah and Harry and their children Ada and Ronnie. *Chicken Soup* shows them between 1936 and 1956, while *Roots* portrays a young farm girl Beatie who has met Ronnie Khan in the city. The play reveals the attitude of her parents when Ronnie comes to visit her at their Norfolk home, eventually deciding not to marry her. The final play, *Jerusalem*, is concerned with Ada Khan and her husband Dave.

Among other occupations, Wesker had been a qualified pastrycook before he became a full-time dramatist, and for his early play *The Kitchen* he drew on the experience gained while working in the kitchens of a Paris restaurant. Wesker's strong social commitment is a major factor in all his plays, as in those of his contemporaries, Pinter and Osborne. As Wesker said:

'The extraordinary thing is that we all happened round about the same time. And Osborne having Jimmy Porter say "There are no more brave causes left" found response in so many of us.'

Carrots with Watercress

2 lbs (2 kg) carrots
1 bunch watercress
½ teaspoon (½ × 5 ml spoon) grated nutmeg
3 tablespoons (3 × 15 ml spoons) double cream
½ oz (15 g) butter
black pepper

Peel the carrots and dice them evenly. Wash and chop the watercress. Boil the carrots in salted water for 10 minutes, or until tender. Drain. Place on a warmed serving dish. Add some black pepper, and dot with butter. Sprinkle the carrots with nutmeg and add the watercress. Stir the cream over the vegetables and serve immediately.

Bob Harris as Troppo, Newton Blick as the tramp, John Warner as Timothy, and Eleanor Drew as Jane. From 'The Tatler', 1954.

Salad Days

The 'musical romp' *Salad Days* was first staged at the Bristol Old Vic Theatre in June 1954, and was the result of collaboration between the musical director Julian Slade and one of the members of the company, Dorothy Reynolds. With an inconsequential plot about two young lovers and Minnie, a magic piano, the musical so delighted audiences in Bristol and Brighton that it was transferred to London. It opened at the Vaudeville Theatre in the Strand on 5 August 1954.

Minnie the piano had everyone on stage dancing, from policeman to bishop. It also entranced audiences, who left the theatre humming snatches of songs including 'We said we wouldn't look back', 'It's easy to sing' and 'Look at me'. John Warner and Eleanor Drew played the young couple, and the original cast included Newton Blick and Pat Heywood as well as the author, Dorothy Reynolds, while Julian Slade performed on one of the two pianos in the orchestra pit.

The critic Milton Shulman was not impressed, but the public seemed to agree with another reviewer who called it 'the freshest and wittiest entertainment seen in London for a long time'. It ran at the Vaudeville for over four years becoming, as Julian Slade put it, 'one of the Strand's most ancient monuments' and earning over £480,000 at the box-office.

Property piano used as Minnie, the magic piano in *Salad Days*.

Lettuce, Avocado and Bacon Salad

1 lettuce
1 ripe avocado
8 oz (225 g) bacon scraps

DRESSING
3 tablespoons (3 × 15 ml spoons) olive oil
1 tablespoon (1 × 15 ml spoon) wine vinegar
1 teaspoon (1 × 5 ml spoon) French mustard
1 teaspoon (1 × 5 ml spoon) sugar
1 clove of garlic, crushed
black pepper
salt

Cut the bacon scraps into small pieces, using kitchen scissors. Discard only very large pieces of rind. Fry the bacon gently in its own fat for about 15 minutes, or until it is crisp and golden brown. Place on kitchen paper to drain. Wipe the lettuce clean. Tear the leaves into smaller pieces and put in a salad bowl. Peel and dice the avocado and mix with the lettuce leaves. Make the dressing by shaking all ingredients together thoroughly in a screw-top jar. Taste, and adjust seasoning if necessary. Immediately before serving, add the dressing. Toss well and sprinkle the crispy bacon scraps over the top.

Potato and Blue Cheese Salad

1 lb (450 g) potatoes – new, when in season
1 lb (450 g) onions
4 oz (100 g) Danish blue cheese

DRESSING
3 tablespoons (3 × 15 ml spoons) plain yogurt
1 tablespoon (1 × 15 ml spoon) wine vinegar
1 teaspoon (1 × 5 ml spoon) lemon juice
1 teaspoon (1 × 5 ml spoon) clear honey
black pepper
salt

Peel the potatoes and cook in boiling salted water until just soft. Peel and slice the onions, separating each slice into onion rings. Dice the cheese and put into a serving bowl with the onions. When cool dice the potatoes and add to onions and cheese. Make the dressing by shaking all the ingredients together thoroughly in a screw-topped jar. Taste and adjust seasoning if necessary. Dress the salad and mix well.

'Oh, Look at Me, I'm Dancing!' from *Salad Days*.

Rice, Chicken and Grape Salad

6 oz (175 g) long grained rice
1 lb (450 g) cooked chicken
8 oz (225 g) black grapes
1 medium green pepper
1 medium red pepper
4 oz (100 g) salted peanuts
¼ pint (150 ml) mayonnaise
black pepper
salt

Cook the rice in boiling, salted water for 15 minutes until it is just soft and not mushy. Drain in a sieve and rinse with boiling water. Leave to cool. Dice the cooked chicken meat. Wash and halve the grapes, removing the pips. Wash the peppers, then remove the seeds and dice the flesh. When the rice is cool, combine all the ingredients, with salt and pepper to taste, reserving a few grapes for decoration. Mix well so that the mayonnaise coats the salad. Decorate with the grapes before serving.

Carrot, Cheese and Orange Salad

2 oranges
black pepper
5 medium carrots
4 oz (100 g) cheddar cheese

Wash the carrots and trim off the tops and tails, peeling them only if they are very dirty. Grate the carrots and cheese into a bowl. Squeeze the juice from half an orange. Add some black pepper and pour the liquid over the grated carrot and cheese. Peel and cut the remaining oranges into small pieces, discarding the pips. Add to the salad, and toss well.

Potato Mountain Salad

2 lbs (1 kg) potatoes
1 medium apple
2 sticks celery
1 onion
1 red pepper
¼ pint (150 ml) vegetable stock
½ oz (15 g) powdered gelatine
¼ pint (150 ml) mayonnaise
black pepper
salt

Peel the potatoes and cook in boiling salted water until just soft. Leave to cool. Peel, core and dice the apple. Slice the celery finely. Peel and chop the onion into small pieces and wash the red pepper. Discard the seeds from the pepper and chop the flesh. Heat the vegetable stock (which can be made with a stock cube) and stir in the gelatine powder until dissolved. Cool. Add the mayonnaise and stir thoroughly. Dice the potatoes, and add all the ingredients to the mayonnaise mixture. Season, adjusting if necessary, and stir well. Pour into a large mould or basin and refrigerate until set. To serve, dip the mould in hot water and invert on to a plate.

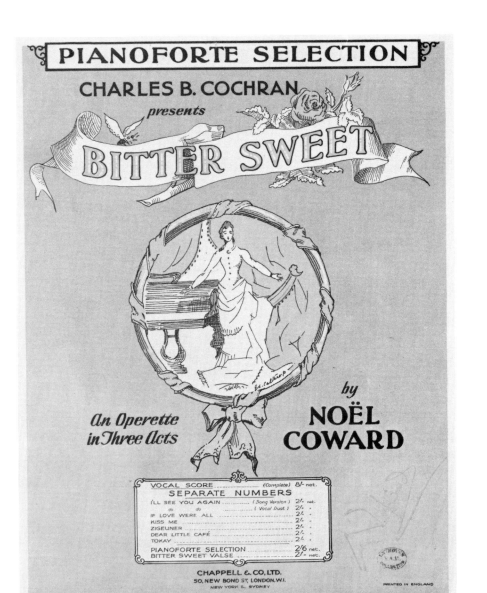

Bitter Sweet

'The idea of Bitter-Sweet was born in the early summer of 1928. It appeared quite unexpectedly . . .'

. . . so Noel Coward reflected on the inspiration for an operetta which was to run at His Majesty's Theatre for 697 performances, originally starring Peggy Wood as Sari Linden. The role had been rejected by Evelyn Laye when it was first offered to her, but having seen the show in London she accepted the part in the New York production, and she subsequently took over from Miss Wood in the West End.

The 'unexpected idea' for *Bitter Sweet* came to Noel Coward when he was staying with friends who played 'Die Fledermaus' on their gramophone:

'Immediately a confused picture of uniforms, bustles, chandeliers and gas-lit cafés formed in my mind, and later, when we were driving over Wimbledon Common, we drew the car to a standstill by the roadside, and in the shade of a giant horse-chestnut tree mapped out roughly the story of Sari Linden. The uniforms, the bustles, chandeliers and gas-lit cafés all fell into place eagerly as though they had been waiting in limbo for just this cue to enter. . . It seemed high time for a little romantic renaissance, and very soon a few of the preliminary melodies began to form in my head.'

That year Coward had to go to America to appear in the New York production of *This Year of Grace*. He wrote the outline of Act I on the voyage, and finished the book in 1929 – the tune for the waltz 'I'll See You Again' coming to him as he sat in a taxi caught in a New York traffic jam.

Rehearsals began in London in May 1929. For its two-week run which opened on 2 July at the Palace Theatre, Manchester, it was a sell-out. In London on 18 July the first night audience at His Majesty's Theatre included the Duke of Kent, Lady Louis Mountbatten and Ivor Novello, and the rapturous applause at the final curtain confirmed Coward's belief that a romantic renaissance was overdue. With designs by Gladys Calthorp and Ernst Stern it was set in 1920s London, late Victorian London, and Vienna in 1880. The entire production was by Coward who must have been justifiably pleased with the glowing review given by James Agate in 'The Sunday Times', 21 July 1929:

'The entire country, so recently as Friday morning, was ringing with the plot of Bitter-Sweet. . . It is cultivated, deft, witty and, above all, tuneful. If butcher-boys do not whistle snatches of it, it will not be the fault of the snatches.'

The Sketch

ONE SHILLING.

WEDNESDAY, SEPTEMBER 4, 1929.

No. 1910.—Vol. CXLVII.

"BITTER-SWEET" CHIC OF 1895: MISS PEGGY WOOD AS SARI.

Miss Peggy Wood wears this lovely costume of the 'nineties in the third act of "Bitter-Sweet," the operette by Noel Coward which Mr. Charles B. Cochran has produced so successfully at His Majesty's. It deals with the life story of Sarah Millick, afterwards Madame Sari Linden, the prima donna, and finally the Marchioness of Shayne. The action ranges from 1929 back to 1875, and onwards to 1895, and Miss Peggy Wood is pictured in her 1895 dress, a splendid example of the fashions of that period—the "Ta-ra-ra Boom-de-ay!"—"leg-of-mutton" sleeves, and bicycle time—which she wears with a superb air. The last act of the operette takes place in the present year.

PHOTOGRAPH BY SASHA, EXCLUSIVE TO "THE SKETCH."

Almond Ice Cream with Raspberry Sauce

ICE CREAM	SAUCE
1 pint (600 ml) milk	2 punnets raspberries or 8 oz (225 g) frozen raspberries
4 oz (100 g) ground almonds	1 tablespoon (1 × 15 ml spoon) brandy
4 egg yolks	caster sugar to taste
4 oz (100 g) caster sugar	
small carton double cream	DECORATION
½ teaspoon (½ × 15 ml spoon) almond essence	8 mint leaves
2 drops green food colouring	4 teaspoons (4 × 5 ml spoons) double cream

Bring the milk to the boil. Reduce the heat and let the milk simmer gently for a minute. Remove from heat. Stir in the ground almonds. Leave for about 30 minutes to let flavours infuse.

Put the egg yolks in a basin with the sugar and whisk until the mixture is pale and creamy. Strain the milk through a fine sieve and add gradually to the egg mixture, whisking all the time. Transfer mixture to a saucepan and cook on a moderate heat, stirring constantly with a wooden spoon until the mixture coats the spoon. Leave to cool.

Keep 4 teaspoons (4 × 5 ml spoons) of double cream for the decoration, and lightly whisk the remaining cream. Fold into the custard mixture. Add the almond essence and food colouring, mixing well. Pour into a shallow container. Put in a deep-freeze. Whisk the mixture once or twice during freezing.

To make the sauce: unfreeze the raspberries (if you are using frozen ones). Liquidise and then strain them, discarding the pips. Add the brandy and a little sugar, but the sauce should be slightly sharp. Chill until ready to serve.

Just before serving, put two scoops of ice cream onto each dessert plate and decorate each with two mint leaves. Carefully spoon some raspberry sauce around the base of the ice cream on each plate. Add a drop of the reserved cream to the sauce on each serving, and with the tip of a knife draw out the cream to a 'squiggle' decoration.

Suggested wine: Vouvray.

Constance Drever and C.H. Workman as Nadina and Lieutenant Bumerli from the cover of 'The Play Pictorial', 1910. Right: cast list from a programme with Margaret Ismay replacing Miss Drever as Nadina.

The Chocolate Soldier

The Chocolate Soldier was first produced in London at the Lyric Theatre on 10 September 1910, with C.H. Workman playing the Swiss Officer Lieutenant Bumerli, and Constance Drever as Nadina who falls in love with him. Oscar Straus's operetta had originally been staged in Vienna in 1908, and the London production, with English words by Stanislaus Stange, followed a successful New York production in 1909.

Since the success of Franz Lehar's operetta *The Merry Widow* at Daly's Theatre in 1907, the vogue for Viennese music had become firmly established in England. English audiences were particularly amused by *The Chocolate Soldier* which was a parody of George Bernard Shaw's play *The Arms and The Man*. Shaw was not at all amused, since dialogue was quoted directly from his original. He did not approve of the way in which the producer F.C. Whitney had conducted the matter, and two months before the opening at the Lyric, Shaw read the English version. He returned it to the theatrical manager J.E. Vedrenne, writing:

'I return the wretched libretto, which is much worse than the original. It is a gross violation of the understanding on which I tolerated the German production. I am not sure that I shall not try to stop it in America. Had I access to the libretto I should certainly have moved when the American run began. Mr Whitney might just as well have approached me and come to an understanding with me: you can see that I am much more reasonable than he has any right to expect me to be. He has behaved as if he were dodging a blackmailer instead of dealing with a decent man of letters.'

Despite Shaw's misgivings, the tuneful operetta was a great success in London and achieved a run of 500 performances.

Chocolate Mint Dessert

½ pint (300 ml) double cream
3 tablespoons (3 × 15 ml spoons) Crème de Menthe
1 packet Cadbury's 'Matchmakers', mint flavour

(this is enough for six people)

Whip the double cream until stiff and add the mint liqueur, mixing thoroughly. Spoon a little of this into the bottom of a small loaf tin and spread it to cover the base. Chop half of the Matchmakers into small pieces and mix with the remaining cream mixture. Pile this into the loaf tin, smoothing the top with a spatula. Cover with foil and freeze for at least 2 hours. To unmould, dip the tin in hot water briefly and invert the tin onto a flat plate. While the surface is slightly soft, decorate the sides and top with the remaining Matchmakers. Chill again before serving.

Suggested wine: A sweet Austrian wine, such as Auslese.

Alfred Drayton, Robertson Hare and Ben Travers (above); Kathleen O'Regan, Carla Lehmann, Olga Lindo and Robert Flemyng (below) in 'Banana Ridge'. Sketches by Rouson from 'The Bystander', 1938.

Banana Ridge

It is suitably paradoxical that Ben Travers, who once declared that he hated food, should have written plays bearing titles 'with edible connections' – *Turkey Time*, Aldwych (1931) *Spotted Dick*, Strand (1939) and *Banana Ridge*, which opened at the Strand Theatre on 27 April 1938.

Banana Ridge, which is set in Malaysia and revolves around riotous paternity complications, was a particular favourite of its author. Before he began his career as a playwright, Travers had spent three years in Singapore and Malacca, working in his father's grocery business. He returned to England in 1911, but his time in the Far East provided him with enough colloquial Malay to write the part of a Chinese servant in *Banana Ridge* more than twenty years later. In the original production Travers played the servant himself, with Robertson Hare looking suitably ridiculous in shorts and solar topee, and Alfred Drayton endlessly hunting a tiger.

Praising the immensely successful production, which achieved 291 performances at the Strand, one reviewer noted that 'the talented author now displays new capacities as an actor, impersonating what may be called a voluble mute.' Travers continued to surprise the critics, writing his last West End play when he was eighty-nine. Freed from the strictures of censorship, *The Bed Before Yesterday* was not a title Travers could have used in the 1930s.

Banana Ridge was successfully revived at the Savoy Theatre in the autumn of 1976, with George Cole and Robert Morley playing roles created by Hare and Drayton.

The equally successful modern master of farce, Alan Ayckbourn, has acknowledged his debt to Travers, telling him in a 'Times' interview of November 1979 that stage-managing some of his plays in rep taught him 'a hell of a lot.' To this Travers replied:

'But we're very lucky; being a comic dramatist is the best career in the world. Especially if you happen to have started in sultanas.'

Baked Bananas with Coconut

4 bananas
2 tablespoons (2 × 15 ml spoons) brown sugar
1 orange
½ lemon
2 tablespoons (2 × 15 ml spoons) rum
2 oz (50 g) shredded coconut

Peel the bananas. Cut them in half lengthwise and place them in a fireproof dish. Squeeze the juice from the half lemon and sprinkle it over the bananas. Squeeze the juice from the orange, and mix with the sugar and rum. Pour this over the bananas, coating them well. Sprinkle the shredded coconut over the bananas and cook in a fairly hot oven (400°F, 200°C, gas mark 6) for 15 minutes.

Serve with cream or ice cream. It is also delicious with honey and whisky whip (see p.119).

Suggested wine: Côteaux du Layon, from the Loire.

LYRIC THEATRE - HAMMERSMITH

Lessees: Associated Theatre Seasons Ltd. Licensee: J. Baxter Somerville
Telephone: RIVerside 4432

Commencing FRIDAY, NOVEMBER 26th, at 7.0   Mats.: Thur. & Sat. at 3.0
Sunday, Nov. 28th, at 7.0 (Members Only)
Evenings at 7.0 (Ex. Nov. 29th)

Tennent Productions Ltd.
in association with the Arts Council of Great Britain
presents

DIANA **CHURCHILL**   ELISABETH **WELCH**

MAX **ADRIAN**

IN

ORANGES AND LEMONS

An intimate revue devised and directed by **LAURIER LISTER**

ANGUS MENZIES   **DENIS MARTIN**
MARJORIE DUNKELS   CHARLOTTE MITCHELL   BRIAN BLADES
ULLA SÖDERBAUM   **NIGEL BURKE**
SILVIA ASHMOLE   JOHN HEAWOOD
DAPHNE PERETZ
ELIZABETH BOYD   ELIZABETH COOPER   SHIRLEY HALL
ANN LYDEKKER   SYLVIA RYE
DAPHNE OXENFORD   **KENNETH CONNOR**
AND
ROSE HILL

At the Pianos: JOHN PRITCHETT and BETTY ROBB
At the Drums: CHRIS BLADES

Choreography by WILLIAM CHAPPELL

A COMPANY OF FOUR PRODUCTION

FOR A LIMITED SEASON ONLY

Diana Churchill, Max Adrian and Elizabeth Welch in 'For Art's Sake', a sketch from *Oranges and Lemons*.

Oranges and Lemons

Oranges and Lemons was originally produced at the Lyric Theatre Hammersmith on 24 November 1948. Glowingly reviewed as 'intellectually sparkling (with more oranges than lemons about)', and 'captivating entertainment, nicely balancing satire and sentiment', it transferred to the Globe Theatre in the following January. It was the second of three outstanding and memorable 'Intimate' revues – the first being *Tuppence Coloured* and the third *Penny Plain* – of which one of the star performers was Joyce Grenfell. She wrote several of the sketches for *Oranges and Lemons* but did not appear in them herself, the unenviable task of replacing her falling to Diana Churchill.

Among other writers who provided the show's thirty-eight sketches and songs were Alan Melville, Sandy Wilson, and Flanders and Swann. The set for a skit called *The Importance of Being Frank* was designed by Cecil Beaton; that for *The Girl from the Opera* was by another now-famous designer, Tanya Moiseiwitsch. Poking fun at a singer hampered by the conventions of Gilbert and Sullivan opera, a Flanders and Swann number was called *In the D'Oyly Cart*, while in *For Art's Sake* Sandy Wilson lampooned Henry Moore's sculptures – a sketch performed by Diana Churchill, Max Adrian and Elizabeth Welch.

Oranges and Lemons, chosen here to introduce an orange and lemon cheesecake, was the title that Noel Coward originally wanted to give to *Bitter Sweet*.

Elizabeth Welch and Max Adrian in 'Snake in the Grass', a sketch from *Oranges and Lemons*.

Orange and Lemon Cheesecake

8 oz (225 g) Philadelphia cream cheese
6 oz (175 g) digestive biscuits
2 oz (50 g) butter
4 oz (100 g) caster sugar
2 egg whites

½ pint (300 ml) double cream
2 oranges
2 lemons
½ oz (15 g) powdered gelatine

(this is enough for six people)

Melt the butter in a saucepan. Crush the biscuits by putting them in a plastic bag and pounding with a rolling pin until they resemble crumbs. Mix the biscuit crumbs well with the melted butter. Lightly grease an 8 in (20 mm) flan dish and put the biscuits in the bottom, pressing down well. Refrigerate while you make the filling.

Cream the Philadelphia cream cheese with the sugar. Whip the double cream until stiff. Grate the rinds of the oranges and lemons and squeeze the juices from both the lemons and 1½ oranges. Slice the remaining half-orange and reserve for decoration. Dissolve the powdered gelatine in the fruit juices and add to the cheese mixture, beating together thoroughly. Whip the egg whites until stiff and fold the double cream and the egg whites into the cheese mixture. Add the grated orange and lemon rinds and pour the cheese mixture over the biscuit base. Chill until firm and decorate with orange slices before serving.

Suggested wine: Barsac.

Pineapple Poll

Set design by Osbert Lancaster for the original production of *Pinapple Poll*. The deck of HMS Hot Cross Bun.

Pineapple Poll, with choreography by John Cranko and music by Sir Arthur Sullivan, was first presented at Sadler's Wells Theatre on 13 March 1951. Cranko had wanted to set a ballet to Sullivan's music since he had first heard his incidental music to *The Tempest*. When the Gilbert and Sullivan copyright expired in November 1950, Cranko thus began selecting tunes from their operas. Arranged by the conductor Charles Mackerras, they included 'Twenty Love-sick Maidens We' from *Patience*, and the 'Chattering Chorus' from *The Pirates of Penzance*.

The scenario for the ballet was inspired by Gilbert's Bab Ballad 'The Bumboat Woman's Story', about Poll Pineapple who falls in love with the handsome Captain Belaye. Not only Poll but all the local girls are enamoured of the dashing Belaye and, disguised as sailors, they try to sail with him in his ship 'HMS Hot Cross Bun'. In his adaptation, Cranko added the characters Blanche, the Captain's fiancée, her mother Mrs Dimple, and Jasper the pot-boy, and he reduced Poll's age to a winsome twenty. The girls' disguise is discovered in the third scene when the 'crew' faint with horror at the Captain's marriage, but all ends happily with Jasper dancing with Poll, and the local Jack Tars reclaiming their wives and girlfriends from the ship.

The delightful sets and costumes for *Pineapple Poll* were designed by Osbert Lancaster. As Peter Williams wrote:

'It is hard to imagine a more suitable designer for a Gilbert and Sullivan inspired work; Lancaster has a lightness of touch and a sense of humour that has its parellel in Gilbert's lyrics.'

With Elaine Fifield as Poll, David Blair as Belaye, and David Poole as Jasper, the new ballet was warmly received by the critics. Clive Barnes' reaction was typical when he noted:

'*Pineapple Poll* is funny, bright, and best of all, exhilarating ... Cranko has not only succeeded in giving the ballet a Gilbertian air of preposterousness and robust whimsy, but also in making this an essentially English romp.'

Pineapple Soufflé

1 large tin pineapple cubes	**3 oz (75 g) caster sugar**
8 oz (225 g) cream cheese	**½ oz (15 g) powdered gelatine**
2 lemons	**¼ pint (150 ml) hot water**
2 oranges	**¼ pint (150 ml) double cream**

Drain the tin of pineapple pieces and reserve ¼ pint (150 ml) of the syrup. Mix the cream cheese with the syrup in a blender. Squeeze the juice from the oranges and lemons, and add to the cheese and syrup mixture. Dissolve the gelatine and sugar in the hot water and add to the cream cheese mixture. Chill this until slightly thickened. Chop the pineapple pieces, reserving a few for decoration. Whip the cream until thick and add the cream and pineapple pieces to the chilled cream cheese mixture, folding together thoroughly. Pour into a medium-sized soufflé dish and decorate with reserved pineapple pieces. Chill until set before serving.

Suggested wine: Sauternes.

Frances Cuka, Avis Bunnage and Murray Melvin in *A Taste of Honey*.

A Taste of Honey

In March 1958 the 19 year-old Sheelagh Delaney went to Manchester to see Terence Rattigan's play *Variations on a Theme*. She left the theatre intent on writing a play which would reflect – more realistically – her own experiences of life in the Manchester suburb of Salford. The resulting manuscript of *A Taste of Honey* so impressed the management of the Theatre Royal, Stratford in East London, that they decided to produce the play immediately. It opened at Stratford East on 27 May 1958, transferred to Wyndham's Theatre on 10 February 1959, and to the Criterion Theatre in June 1959, achieving a total run of 349 performances.

A Taste of Honey concerns a teenage girl from Salford, played by Frances Cuka, who is left alone by her mother (Avis Bunnage). She meets and lives with a coloured sailor, who abandons her when she becomes pregnant. Befriended by a homosexual (Murray Melvin), she is relatively happy until her mother reappears and forces the boy to leave.

The success of *A Taste of Honey* owed much to Joan Littlewood's production, with its starkly monochrome set, jazz trio and 'asides' to the audience. Critics remarked on the Music Hall influences in the production, a comparison which Miss Littlewood acknowledged to be correct. She had in fact formed the Theatre Workshop in 1954 expressly to produce plays which the working classes would enjoy; plays that were 'grand, vulgar, simple, pathetic – but not genteel, not poetical.'

Whisky and Honey Whip

2 egg yolks
3 oz (75 g) Philadelphia cream cheese
1 oz (50 g) caster sugar
½ pint (300 ml) double cream
2 tablespoons (2 × 15 ml spoons) clear honey
2 tablespoons (2 × 15 ml spoons) whisky

(this is enough for six people)

Whisk the egg yolks and caster sugar together in a bowl over a pan of hot water until the mixture is pale and very thick. Combine the cream cheese, honey and whisky in a blender until smooth and mix with the egg and sugar mixture. Beat the cream until it is stiff and stands in peaks, and fold this into the honey mixture. Spoon into serving dishes and chill until ready to serve. Langue de chat biscuits go well with this.

Suggested wine: Asti Spumante.

Avis Bunnage and Frances Cuka as mother and daughter. Cartoon by Glan Williams from 'The Tatler', 1959.

Elizabeth Robson and Adrian de Peyer as the Princess and the Prince in *The Love of Three Oranges*.

The Love of Three Oranges

A light concoction of pantomime, circus and fairy-tale, with dashes of magic and mime and a good measure of ingenious staging, Prokofiev's comic opera *The Love of Three Oranges* opened at Sadler's Wells theatre in April 1963. It was the first time that a Prokofiev opera had been produced in London.

Commissioned in 1919 by the Chicago Opera Company, it was first performed by them in 1921. It tells the story (originally written by Gozzi) of a prince who can only be cured of his deep melancholy by being made to laugh. The witch Fata Morgana thwarts all attempts to cure him until she falls over, thereby accidentally provoking his laughter and his salvation. The opera also concerns the prince's adventures during his search for three oranges, in one of which is hidden the princess of his dreams. Prokofiev loved the fantastic and the grotesque, and his score perfectly reflects those elements of the story.

The original British production of *A Love of Three Oranges* was by the New Opera Company who from 1960 collaborated with the Sadler's Wells Opera so that successful productions could be taken into the Sadler's Wells repertoire. The 1963 production, imaginatively directed by Peter Coe, was conducted by the New Opera's musical director, Leon Lovett. The choruses of both companies took part. Among the principal singers were Adrian de Peyer as the Prince; Julian Moyle as Pantaloon, Rita Hunter as Fata Morgana, and Elizabeth Robson as Princess Ninette. The 'Times' critic wrote of the first night performance at Sadler's Wells:

'... it is one of Prokofiev's freshest scores and once Mr Leon Lovett gets the orchestra moving just a little more fluently, it should prove irresistible; it is already enormous fun.'

A recent successful revival, opening at Glyndebourne on 25 May 1982, was produced by Frank Corsaro and featured spectacular designs by Maurice Sendak.

Orange Cream Pie

ORANGE SHORTCRUST PASTRY
6 oz (175 g) plain flour
3 oz (75 g) butter
2 tablespoons (2 × 15 ml spoons) water
juice of ½ orange
grated peel of 1 orange

(This is enough for six people)

FILLING
3 oranges
juice of ½ lemon
½ oz (15 g) powdered gelatine
3 tablespoons (3 × 15 ml spoons) cold water
2 eggs
4 oz (100 g) caster sugar
¼ pint (150 ml) double cream

To make the pastry, sieve the flour into a bowl; add the butter cut into small pieces, and rub it into the flour with the fingertips until the mixture resembles breadcrumbs. Grate the peel of one orange and add to the bowl. Pour the 2 tablespoons (2 × 15 ml spoons) water into the bowl with the juice of half an orange and blend with fork into a dough. Place on a lightly floured surface and knead gently. Leave in a cool place for 15 minutes before rolling with a lightly floured rolling pin and lining a 7 in (18 mm) flan dish. Bake blind for 30 minutes, for the first 10 minutes in a fairly hot oven (400°F, 200°C, gas mark 6) and then lowering the heat for the remaining 20 minutes to 375°F, 190°C, gas mark 5). Remove the beans or rice used to bake blind, and allow the pastry case to cool.

For the filling, grate the two remaining oranges and lemon and squeeze the juice from these and the other half orange. Disssolve the gelatine in the cold water. Separate the eggs, reserving the egg whites, and beat the egg yolks with the caster sugar in a bowl over a pan of hot water until thick and pale. Add the orange and lemon juice and continue cooking until the mixture thickens. Remove from the heat and beat in the rinds and the dissolved gelatine. Whip the egg whites until stiff and fold in the orange and cream mixture. Spoon the filling into the pastry case and chill before serving.

Suggested wine: Moselle Spätlese.

'Sweet Georgia Brown' performed by Helen Galzer, Newton Winters and David Cameron.

Bubbling Brown Sugar

With verve and vitality, high octane choreography by Billy Wilson and a superb performance by the leggy Helen Gelzer, the musical *Bubbling Brown Sugar* sizzled to life on the stage of the Royalty Theatre on 28 September 1977.

A nostalgic trip to the night clubs of Harlem between the years 1920 and 1940, the show featured jazz classics including 'Ain't Misbehavin', 'Honeysuckle Rose', 'Sweet Georgia Brown', 'Solitude' and 'God Bless the Child'. Billy Daniels acted as the guide on this musical tour, performing numbers with Elaine Delmar and Lon Satton. Satton, associate producer of *Bubbling Brown Sugar*, followed his rôle in that show by creating the part of the roller-skating Poppa in Lloyd-Webber's *Starlight Express*.

The energy exuded by the cast of *Bubbling Brown Sugar* should have been bottled and sold in the theatre foyer with the cast recording. The final number, 'It Doesn't Mean a Thing', brought the curtains down to frenzied applause after the performance by white-suited men and girls topping and twirling in toppers, fishnet tights and silver shoes, brought the show to a close. In the best vaudeville tradition, Helen Gelzer, who had begun her career singing telegrams for Western Union, was instantly declared A Star and was fêted by the press. The show which had brought live entertainment back to the Royalty Theatre for the first time in three years, kept enthusiastic audiences coming to Portugal Street for the next 18 months. After having changed hands several times since *Bubbling Brown Sugar* closed in 1979, the Royalty is currently owned by Stoll Moss Theatres, bringing live performances once more to its stage.

Burnt Sugar Apricots

1 large tin apricot halves　　**2 oz (50 g) caster sugar**
½ pint (300 ml) double cream　　**2 oz (50 g) soft brown sugar**

Drain the apricot halves and arrange them, cut side-down, in a shallow fireproof dish. Beat the cream and the caster sugar together until the mixture is thick. Spread this carefully over the apricots, covering them completely and smoothing the surface with a spatula. Put foil or cling-film over the dish and freeze for about an hour, or until the cream is frozen. Pre-heat a grill to its fiercest heat for about 5 minutes, then uncover the dish and sprinkle the brown sugar over the cream, completely covering the surface. Grill for about 2 minutes until the sugar is bubbling and caramelised. Cool, and refrigerate again before serving.

Suggested wine: A sweet, sparkling white wine.

Costume designs by Tanya Moiseiwitsch for Faith Brook as Charlotta and for Edith Evans as Madame Ravensky, New Theatre, 1948.

The Cherry Orchard

The Cherry Orchard by Anton Chekhov was first produced in London by the Incorporated Stage Society at the Aldwych Theatre on 28 May 1911. The Stage Society, like its predecessor the Independent Theatre, was formed specifically to present experimental British and foreign plays, and it helped to establish the work of Shaw (see p.30) as well as Ibsen (see p.81), Somerset Maugham, Arnold Bennett, Tolstoy and Turgenev. They produced plays on Sunday afternoons so that professional actors could appear in them. By 1914 they also gave Monday matinées, and they continued actively untl 1939.

The Moscow Art Theatre, formed by the collaboration of Nemirovich-Danchenko and Stanislavsky, had staged the original production of *The Cherry Orchard* in 1904. Chekhov's association with the Art Theatre had begun during its first season (1898) when they presented *The Seagull*, and his plays became so identified with this company that they adopted a seagull as their emblem. Like *The Three Sisters* (1901) Chekhov wrote the complex but seemingly naturalistic *The Cherry Orchard* specially for the company at the Art Theatre.

The Stage Society production was remarkable only in as much as it was the first time that the play had been seen on the London stage. For an effective presentation of Chekhov's subtle and symbolic play, English audiences had to wait until 1926 when Komisarjevsky produced it at the Barnes Theatre, perfectly understanding the atmosphere that Chekhov had created.

One of the most notable productions in the play's history was that of a version by John Gielgud, performed by the Royal Shakespeare Company at the Aldwych in December 1961. Produced by Michel Saint-Denis it boasted an incomparable cast-list: Peggy Ashcroft as Madame Ranevsky, Judi Dench as Anya, Dorothy Tutin as Varya, John Gielgud as Gaev, Patience Collier as Charlotta Ivanovna, and Ian Holm as Trofimov. Two reviews sum up the general enthusiasm which the first night performance generated:

'A rich, warm glow lit up the West End sky last night.'
'The Royal Shakespeare Company at the Aldwych has given London the nicest kind of Christmas present.'

A more recent West End production of the play opened at the Haymarket Theatre in October 1983. It starred Frank Finlay and Joan Plowright, and the cast included Joanna David, Bernard Miles, Leslie Phillips and Bill Fraser.

Judi Dench as Anya with George Murcell as Lopahin.

Dorothy Tutin as Varya, John Gielgud as Gaev and Judi Dench as Anya.

Drunken Cherry Ice Cream with Hot Sauce

1 large tin black cherries
1 lb (450 g) block dairy ice cream
3 tablespoons (3 × 15 ml spoons) brandy
1 tablespoon (1 × 15 ml spoon) cornflour
1 tablespoon (1 × 15 ml spoon) water

Drain the syrup from the tin of cherries and reserve it for the sauce. Remove the stones from the cherries and chop the flesh into very small pieces. Put the cherries into a bowl, pour the brandy over them, and leave for at least an hour. Put the block of ice cream into another bowl and break up with a fork. Drain the cherries again, adding the brandy liquid to the cherry syrup. Mix the cherries well with the ice cream; pour into a small soufflé dish and freeze to set the ice cream again.

To make the cherry sauce, put the cherry syrup into a saucepan and make up to ½ pint (300 ml) with water. Heat gently. Mix the cornflour with a tablespoon (1 × 15 ml spoon) of water in a cup. Add a little hot cherry syrup and, when smooth, return cornflour mixture to the saucepan. Stir over a low heat until the mixture thickens. Taste, adding a little sugar if necessary, and serve the sauce with the ice cream.

Suggested wine: Muscat de Beaunes de Venise.

Picture credits

BBC Hulton Picture Library *pages 72 (right), 86*; Rexton S. Bunnett *page 32*; Charles Castle *page 44 (right)*; Donald Cooper *page 122 (bottom)*; Derek de Marney *page 102*; De Wynters Ltd *page 122 (top)*; Dominic Photography *pages 48, 96, 118 (bottom), 120, 122 (bottom)*; Ellis & Walery *pages 63-64*; Bertram Park *page 94*; Houston Rogers *pages 75, 76 (top and centre), 82, 126, 127*; David Sim *page 35*; Stage Photo Co. *pages 70, 90*; Reg Wilson *page 50*.

Our thanks are also due to the following for permission to reproduce the illustrations listed below:
Ursula Haselden *page 91*; International Music Publishers *pages 84, 104*; Tanya Moiseiwitsch *page 124*; John Murray Publishers Ltd *page 116*; Theatre Museum *Frontispiece and decorative devices on the pages preceding the recipes, pages 12, 15, 18, 22-26, 30, 33-38, 40-42, 44 (left), 46, 52, 54, 56, 58-60, 62-64, 66, 68, 70-72 (left), 74-78, 80, 82, 88-90, 92, 94, 98-100, 102, 106, 108, 110, 112-114, 116, 118 (top: left and right), 119, 126-127; endpiece.*